Old Testament
Commentary Survey

Old Testament Commentary Survey

Tremper Longman III

BAKER BOOK HOUSE
Grand Rapids, Michigan 49516

Copyright 1991 by
Baker Book House Company

Printed in the United States of America

Library of Congress Cataloging-in-Publication Data

Longman, Tremper.
    Old Testament commentary survey / Tremper Longman III.
        p.   cm.
    ISBN 0-8010-5670-5
    1. Bible. O.T.—Commentaries—Bibliography. I. Title.
Z7772.A1L64
[BS1171.2]
016.2217—dc20   91-21584
                                                                        CIP

To

Murali Rao

Lover of Books

Supporter of Scholarship

Friend

Contents

Acknowledgments

When I began this project several years ago, I thought it would take a minimum amount of time and serve a limited readership. Many of my students had asked for my opinion on commentaries, but one of them, Eric Brauer, now a minister in Dublin, kept pestering me to compile a list and make it available in our seminary bookstore. I figured I could devote a few minutes each day to writing up a brief review of the best commentaries I knew on certain biblical books. To make a long story short, Allan Fisher, director of publications at Baker Book House, caught wind of my efforts and asked me to expand the list to include yet more commentaries and also other reference books to serve as the Old Testament counterpart to Don Carson's *New Testament Commentary Series* (3d ed., 1986). I did not realize how much work was involved; but now that it is over, I would like to express my appreciation to both Eric and Allan for their encouragement to write this guide.

The process of collecting the volumes for review has led me to an even greater appreciation for our library at Westminster Theological Seminary. We are blessed with both a full collection of books and a wonderful library staff. In particular I would like to thank Grace Mullen, Jane Patete, Jean

Belmonte, and Denise Pakala for their professionalism and help during this project. I also enjoyed the considerable help of our bookstore staff, including David Lauten, Don Strickland, Bobby Sutherland, and Charles Roberts. Last but not least, I appreciate the work of Dean Ulrich, one of my current Ph.D. students, who aided me in checking a number of references. Thank you all.

Finally, I wish to dedicate this book to my wife Alice, and our three children, Tremper IV, Timothy, and Andrew.

Abbreviations

AB	Anchor Bible
ANET	*Ancient Near Eastern Texts Relating to the Old Testament*
BDB	Brown-Driver-Briggs, *Hebrew and English Lexicon of the Old Testament*
BSC	*Bible Student's Commentary*
BST	*The Bible Speaks Today*
CBC	*The Cambridge Bible Commentary*
CC	*Communicator's Commentary*
DSB	*The Daily Study Bible*
EBC	*Expositor's Bible Commentary*
FOTL	*Forms of Old Testament Literature*
GKC	Gesenius-Kautzsch-Cowley, *Gesenius' Hebrew Grammar*
IB	*The Interpreter's Bible*
ICC	*The International Critical Commentary*
Interp	*Interpretation*
ITC	*International Theological Commentary*
KB	Koehler-Baumgartner, *Lexicon in Veteris Testamenti Libros*

NCB	*New Century Bible*
NICOT	*The New International Commentary on the Old Testament*
NIVEC	*The NIV Exhaustive Concordance*
OTL	*Old Testament Library*
OTM	*Old Testament Message*
TBC	*Torch Bible Commentaries*
TDOT	*Theological Dictionary of the Old Testament*
TI	*Text and Interpretation*
TOTC	*Tyndale Old Testament Commentaries*
WBC	*Word Biblical Commentary*
WEC	*Wycliffe Exegetical Commentary*

Introduction

Of making many books there is no end, and much study wearies the body. (Eccles. 12:12)

While surveying the many commentaries and other reference books listed in this guide, this verse came to mind more than once. Sometimes it seemed as if a new commentary appeared every week!

Upon more rational reflection, however, it is clear that in fact there is a real dearth of commentaries on the Old Testament. This situation is not simply the result of the fact that many commentaries are of little real worth, but also because there are only a few good commentaries on the books of the Old Testament. Furthermore, no single commentary, no matter how exhaustive, can hope to provide all the information the reader might want and need. In addition, commentaries are addressed to specialized audiences. A commentary that is written with the needs of the layperson in mind will often not be of real interest to the scholar, while one written for a scholarly audience is often of no use to the layperson. Ministers have enough training to be interested in answers to technical questions, but also want help in making the text relevant to the people in their congregation.

Who Should Read This Guide?

There are many commentaries available. As a specialist in Old Testament, I do not think I have been asked any question more frequently than "What's the best commentary on . . . ?"

This guide is for anyone, layperson or minister, who desires to buy a commentary. It lists a number of works available for each book of the Old Testament, gives a brief indication of their emphases and viewpoints, and evaluates them. This guide will be helpful to seminary students who are beginning to build the reference library that will be crucial to their preaching and teaching ministries.

The Evaluation

Some might disagree with me in terms of the value I assign to individual commentaries. It is accordingly of some interest to know what I value in a commentary and the perspective from which I write.

I represent an evangelical approach to the Old Testament, and, accordingly, give high marks to good commentaries that come from a similar perspective. However, it is important to emphasize the adjective "good." I am particularly hard on shallow or incompetent commentaries that come from the perspective I advocate. Similarly, I can appreciate and learn from writers who write from a perspective different than my own.

I evaluate commentaries on a 1 to 5 scale. One or two asterisks indicate that the commentary is inferior or deficient and I discourage its purchase. Four or five is a high mark. Three, obviously, means a commentary is good but not great.

I also indicate who would most benefit from the commentary under consideration. There are three categories that I distinguish: L(ayperson); M(inister) (seminary students should consider themselves in this category); and S(cholar).

If you are interested in building a basic Old Testament reference library, I recommend purchases based on certain budget restraints. This budget guide has the seminary student in mind, but will also be helpful for laypeople and ministers.

For a similar guide to the New Testament, please consult D. A. Carson, *New Testament Commentary Survey* (3d ed., Baker, 1986). If your bookstore does not carry Carson's survey or any book that you want, remember that most Christian bookstores can special order books and get them to you within a week or two.

The Scope of the Guide

There are countless reference books on the Old Testament, especially if out-of-print books are taken into account. It has been particularly difficult to determine what to include in this survey. However, the best books I know have all been included.

The survey has two main parts. First, noncommentary reference books are listed. Besides commentaries, a basic Old Testament library should include an introduction, theology, and history of the Old Testament. An atlas of the Old Testament world helps readers visualize the stories they are reading. More advanced students of the Bible will also be interested in reference works for the Hebrew text and other background material. The second part of the survey—the commentary guide—is the longest. There are three sections in this part. In the first section, I provide a list of commentary series and make some general comments. The series authored by one or two people are evaluated at this point. Those with multiple authors are described in the first part, but evaluated in the third. In the second section, I evaluate a select number of one-volume commentaries. In the third section, I evaluate individual commentaries on each biblical book.

I list not only bibliographical information for each book but also its length and price (except when I was unable to locate a reliable indication). Of course, publishers often raise prices from year to year, so it is important to check the price of a book before you actually purchase it.

I plan to provide periodic updates to this survey. If you have any comments or reactions, please feel free to contact me at the following address:

Tremper Longman III
Westminster Theological Seminary
P.O. Box 27009
Philadelphia, PA 19118

The Use and Abuse of Commentaries

There is a right way and a wrong way to use a commentary. Actually, there are two wrong ways. The first is to ignore completely the use of commentaries. Some people do not consult commentaries because they believe that, since all Christians are equal as they approach the Scriptures, scholars have no privileged insight into the biblical text. The second error is to become overly dependent on commentaries. "These people have devoted their whole lives to the study of the Bible. How can my opinion measure up to theirs?"

Those holding the first position are wrong because they forget that God gives different gifts to different people in the church. Not all people are equally adept at understanding the Bible and teaching it to others (1 Cor. 12:12–31). Those holding the second position err in the opposite direction. They forget that God has given believers the Spirit by which they can discern spiritual things (1 Cor. 2:14–16).

The right way to use a commentary is as a help. We should first of all study a passage without reference to any helps. Only after coming to an initial understanding of the passage should we consult commentaries.

Neither should we let commentaries bully us. Many times they will be of great help, but sometimes the reader will be right and they will be wrong.

Old Testament Reference Works

Introductions

Archer, G. L., Jr. *A Survey of Old Testament Introduction.* Moody, 1964 (rev. 1974). 507 pp. $16.95 hb.

Certainly the most conservative introduction on the list, it takes a more apologetic and polemical perspective than other evangelical introductions. Nonetheless, Archer is very well informed and much value may be gained from reading this introduction. Much of the book is dated. LM***

Childs, B. S. *Introduction to the Old Testament as Scripture.* Fortress, 1979. 688 pp. $31.95 hb.

One of the most-discussed books of the 1980s. Childs uses the introductory format to present his "canonical approach." This approach asks what function the individual books serve in their final form in their present context within the Scripture of the church. As a result, there is a great deal of theology in this introduction. There is also less discussion of the history of research and the results of critical methodology. However, this does not mean that Childs rejects historical-critical methods; he merely brackets them (for the most part). Imminently worthwhile and stimulating. Geared for seminary-level classroom use. MS*****

Craigie, P. C. *The Old Testament: Its Background, Growth, and Content*. Abingdon, 1986. 351 pp. $23.75 hb.

This introduction is actually two books in one. It surveys the books of the Old Testament like a standard introduction, but also provides a brief history. Indeed, one of the problems with the book is that it is too brief, covering only a small selection of topics, and these too superficially. However, the volume may be useful to college students and laypeople. L*

Eissfeldt, O. *The Old Testament: An Introduction*. Trans. P. R. Ackroyd. Harper and Row, 1965. xxiv/861 pp. $14.95 pb.

Eissfeldt's introduction is a classic of the critical school, containing many of the opinions of traditional historical criticism. In it, we encounter a full exposition of source analysis of the Pentateuch. That Eissfeldt is not a pure traditionalist, however, is immediately evident when he posits an L stratum to the Pentateuch. Eissfeldt's introduction follows the growth of the text from the preliterary stage through the literary prehistory to the canonical form of the text to the transmission of the text. Erudite and well-written. S****

Gottwald, N. K. *The Hebrew Bible: A Socio-Literary Introduction*. Fortress, 1985. xxx/702 pp. $21.95 pb.

Gottwald established himself in the field of sociological interpretation of the Bible with his lengthy and controversial study of the premonarchical period of Israel (*The Tribes of*

Yahweh). This volume applies his sociological approach with literary insights to the study of the whole canon in an introductory format. Definitely for seminary level and up. MS***

✕   Harrison, R. K. *Introduction to the Old Testament.* Eerdmans, 1969. 1325 pp. $34.95 hb.

One of the most complete introductions. It has a definite proclivity for historical issues, as opposed to literary and theological ones. There is a heavy emphasis on history of research. It shows the erudition and competency of the author and is an admirable reference tool. It is a little too heavy for classroom use and is dated. MS***

Kaiser, O. *Introduction to the Old Testament: A Presentation of Its Results and Problems.* Trans. J. Sturdy. Augsburg, 1975 (1st Ger. ed. 1969). xvii/420 pp.

This short, readable introduction presents critical German Old Testament scholarship to the interested reader. It is not as full as Eissfeldt, but more up to date. MS***

Laffey, A. L. *An Introduction to the Old Testament: A Feminist Perspective.* Fortress, 1988. 240 pp. $12.95 pb.

As the subtitle indicates, this book is not a traditional introduction. It intends to serve as a supplement to such introductions in the classroom. It surveys the Old Testament with an eye to stories and issues that concern women. There is definitely a place for such an endeavor. While Laffey is not overly radical, it is to be regretted that she distorts, misinterprets, and even contradicts herself as she mines the Old Testament text with the purpose of raising our feminist consciousness. M***

Lasor, W. S., D. A. Hubbard, and F. W. Bush. *Old Testament Survey.* Eerdmans, 1982. xiii/696 pp. $24.95 hb.

This distinguished trio of biblical scholars from Fuller Theological Seminary has produced a readable introduction suitable for classroom use at the seminary level. They interact with recent scholarship and provide what might be called a "progressive evangelical" perspective on the various books of the Old Testament. LM****

Rendtorff, R. *The Old Testament: An Introduction.* Fortress, 1986. xi/308 pp. $24.95 hb.

Like Craigie, Rendtorff surveys both history and literature in this short volume. Indeed, he merges his concern with the history, institutions, and literature of Old Testament times into a single volume. He reconstructs the history of Israel primarily from the texts themselves, only rarely using archeological data. He is skeptical of the text's ability to inform us accurately about the earliest periods of time. Thus, he disregards the Book of Joshua's evidence that Palestine was occupied through conquest, preferring instead to speak of settlement. In the last section, the introduction proper, Rendtorff takes a moderately critical approach. He rejects the Documentary Hypothesis of the Pentateuch, opting instead for a tradition-historical approach to the growth of the first five books of the Bible. Rendtorff has been heavily influenced by Childs' canonical approach to the Old Testament. MS***

Soggin, J. A. *Introduction to the Old Testament.* OTL. Westminster, 1976. xxxii/510 pp. $27.50 hb.

A translation of an Italian original that was published in 1974. A critical introduction heavily influenced by German scholarship, it includes an analysis of the intertestamental books. It deals first with the Pentateuch (displaying the traditional four-source theory) and the Former Prophets. The prophets are presented in chronological order and then the writings. Soggin's discussion of many issues seems too short and superficial. S**

Young, E. J. *An Introduction to the Old Testament.* Eerdmans, 1949 (rev. 1984). 456 pp. $15.95 hb.

Young, late professor of Old Testament at Westminster Theological Seminary, presents an erudite but brief introduction. While consistently conservative, Young does not back off from nontraditional interpretations (e.g., his argument that Ecclesiastes was not authored by Solomon). Still worthwhile, the book is nonetheless dated. LM***

Theology

Clements, R. E. *Old Testament Theology: A Fresh Approach.* John Knox, 1976. x/214 pp.

This is a good, reliable introduction to the discipline and content of Old Testament theology. Clements divides his discussion along the lines of general topics like "The God of Israel" and "The People of God." He writes clearly. LM***

De Graaf, S. G. *Promise and Deliverance.* 4 vols. Presbyterian and Reformed, 1977–81.

De Graaf's four volumes (originally published in Dutch) cover the entire Scriptures; the first two are dedicated to the Old Testament. De Graaf studies the Old Testament with an eye on the covenant and the kingdom of God. The book is written in an easy-to-understand style. LM****

✗   Hasel, G. *Old Testament Theology: Basic Issues in the Current Debate*. Eerdmans, 1972 (3d ed. 1982). 168 pp. $7.95 pb.

This handy volume brings order to the rather complex issue of the theology of the Old Testament. When Hasel wrote in the early 1970s the discipline was in transition with no clear consensus view, a situation that has only intensified in the past two decades. Since a number of the theologians he discusses are still very relevant (Eichrodt, von Rad, and Childs, for instance), Hasel's guide is still very helpful. LM***

Kaiser, W. C., Jr. *Toward an Old Testament Theology*. Zondervan, 1978. 303 pp. $17.95 hb.

Kaiser attempts a thematic study of God's promise to his people from the creation texts through the Old Testament into the New. He gives us a very interesting picture of one important theme in the Bible. LM****

Laurin, R. B. (ed.). *Contemporary Old Testament Theologians*. Judson, 1970. 223 pp.

This volume presents a collection of essays that describe and analyze the thought of seven recent Old Testament theologians: Eichrodt, von Rad, Procksch, Vriezen, Jacob, Knight, and van Imschoot. M***

Martens, E. A. *God's Design: A Focus on Old Testament Theology*. Baker, 1981. 368 pp. $12.95 hb./$9.95 pb.

Martens presents an admirable and profitable study of the theme of God's plan of salvation. He traces this theme through the Old Testament into the New. He has not discovered the "center" of Old Testament theology as he claims, but gives evidence to one of the signs of the unity of biblical revelation. LM****

Payne, J. Barton. *The Theology of the Older Testament.* Zondervan, 1962. 554 pp. $19.95 pb.

This book presents Payne's distinctive focus on covenant, which he redefines as "last will and testament." Payne reasons that since Christ died only once there is only one testament (contra dispensationalism), although there are two aspects: an older aspect that *anticipates* Christ's death and a new aspect that *celebrates* Christ's death. Payne is quite polemical toward critical approaches and ignores them for the most part. He takes a synchronic and systematic theological approach to the subject. LM**

Rad, G. von. *Old Testament Theology.* 2 vols. Harper and Row, 1962–65. 480 pp. $19.95 hb. (ea.).

This set was the focus of attention throughout the 1960s and early 1970s. It still exercises tremendous influence as one of the seminal studies of this century. It was a reaction against Eichrodt's theology, although they share some traits in common. Von Rad's approach is diachronic—he studies traditions as they develop and are applied (reactualized) from generation to generation. Von Rad's *Wisdom in Israel* (Abingdon, 1972) is also well worth studying. MS****

Robertson, O. P. *The Christ of the Covenants.* Presbyterian and Reformed, 1981. 308 pp. $9.95 pb.

Robertson gives an accurate and incredibly clear account of the concept and development of the covenant idea through the Old Testament and into the New. This treatment is the best description of this important biblical concept that a reader can buy. LM*****

Schmidt, W. H. *The Faith of the Old Testament: A History.* Trans. J. Sturdy. Westminster, 1983. x/302 pp. $25.00 hb./$12.95 pb.

This book is somewhere between a theology of the Old Testament and a history of Israel's religion. The author takes a critical approach to the issues. He discusses many of the current debates concerning the development of Israel's religion. M**

Terrien, S. *The Elusive Presence: Toward a New Biblical Theology.* Harper and Row, 1978. 544 pp. $13.95 pb.

One of the most perplexing questions that biblical theology poses is the question of the center of the message of the Bible. It is around this center that a presentation of theology takes place. The most popular answer to this question in the past few decades is the covenant. Terrien posits over against the covenant the idea of God's elusive presence. God's presence gives meaning to life, but the Old Testament bears witness that God is also a "self-concealing" God, not to be manipulated by his creatures. Terrien thus provides a stimulating study of the presence of God in the Scriptures. MS****

Histories of Israel

Ackroyd, P. *Exile and Restoration.* OTL. Westminster, 1968. 302 pp. $14.95 hb.

Although not a survey of the entire history of Israel, this volume covers a critical period, the sixth century B.C., when

Israel was in Babylonian captivity. It also narrates the beginnings of the return and rebuilding after the Persian conquest of Babylon. It is something of a classic study written from a critical perspective. MS***

Anderson, B. W. *Understanding the Old Testament.* 4th ed. Prentice-Hall, 1986. xxi/649 pp. $36.33 hb.

This is a popular college textbook. The approach is moderately critical. The book is nicely produced, with a number of illustrations and photographs. The first edition appeared in 1957. Anderson integrates "historical and archeological research, literary criticism and biblical theology" (p. xix). He begins with the exodus as the start of historical consciousness. LM****

Bright, J. *A History of Israel.* 3d ed. Westminster, 1981. 528 pp. $18.95 hb.

Bright's history is well known and well used in the seminary classroom. His approach is moderately critical, in the tradition of W. F. Albright and G. E. Wright. In other words, it is more optimistic than the German tradition in terms of reconstructing Israel's early history. Bright integrates Near Eastern material and archeological investigations. His generally positive approach to the history of Israel, however, should not blind the reader to the fact that he often goes against the text in his description of biblical events like the exodus and the settlement. He has good maps and excellent chronological charts. MS****

Davis, J. J., and J. C. Whitcomb. *A History of Israel: From Conquest to Exile.* Baker, 1980. 542 pp. $17.95 hb.

Davis and Whitcomb describe the history of Israel by simply retelling the biblical story and throwing in some archeological facts here and there. The volume may have some value for novices and high school students. L*

Gottwald, N. K. *The Tribes of Yahweh: A Sociology of the Religion of Liberated Israel, 1250–1050 B.C.* Orbis, 1979. 944 pp. $24.95 pb.

This book covers the conquest and period of the judges using the sociological method. Gottwald's distinctive methodological approach will strike most as wrongheaded (the dedication to the people of North Vietnam is the first hint), but he is upfront about it and many significant insights are found in the book. S***

Hayes, J. H., and J. Maxwell Miller (eds.). *Israelite and Judaean History.* Westminster, 1977. 542 pp.

A multiauthor volume in which each scholar addresses a particular period. Some of the scholars (e.g., William Dever and T. L. Thompson) are known for their skeptical attitude toward the reconstruction of early Israelite history. This volume is more in line with German historical work (in the tradition of Noth and Alt) than, for instance, with Bright, and thus is more critical toward the text. MS***

Hayes, J. H., and J. Maxwell Miller. *A History of Ancient Israel and Judah.* Westminster/John Knox, 1986. 524 pp. $27.95 hb.

The approach taken to the history of Israel is moderately critical in that the authors neither accept the history that the text presents at face value nor reject it out of hand. The writing is clear and easy to follow. M****

Herrmann, S. *A History of Israel in Old Testament Times.* 2d ed. Fortress, 1981. 440 pp. $29.95 pb.

A relatively brief but comprehensive history of Israel. It was originally published in 1973 in German, under the influence of Alt and Noth. The second edition covers Israel's history to 63 B.C.; otherwise there are no substantial changes. MS***

Jagersma, H. *A History of Israel in the Old Testament Period.* Fortress, 1983. 304 pp. $15.95 pb.

This volume is a translation (by John Bowden) of a Dutch work first published in 1979. Jagersma approaches the biblical account of Israel's past with great skepticism and will believe nothing without outside confirmation. The book is very brief and clearly written. A second volume covers the period from Alexander the Great to Bar Kochba (ca. 350 B.C.–A.D. 150). MS***

Merrill, E. H. *Kingdom of Priests: A History of Old Testament Israel.* Baker, 1987. 546 pp. $24.95 hb.

Merrill has written a chronologically comprehensive survey of Israel's history from a decidedly conservative perspective. There has been a great need for a suitable seminary-level textbook in this area and this volume will fill the gap at least temporarily. Its weakness is that it often merely paraphrases the biblical story, throwing in some interesting archeological and Near Eastern facts. It highlights chronology, giving absolute dates for early history—a dubious enterprise. LM***

Merrill, E. H. *An Historical Survey of the Old Testament.* Baker, 1966. 348 pp. $9.95 pb.

This volume is too superficial for seminary-level instruction. Merrill's *Kingdom of Priests*, in spite of its faults, is a vastly superior work. However, the publisher continues to reprint this volume along with the more recent one. Now twenty years old, it should probably be discontinued. The positions taken in the volume are not well argued, and the tone is dogmatic and polemical. L*

Schultz, S. J. *The Old Testament Speaks.* 4th ed. Harper and Row, 1980. 448 pp. $24.95 hb.

This is the conservative equivalent to the college textbook by Anderson. As opposed to Anderson, who begins with the exodus, Schultz starts with the creation accounts and treats them as serious history. He utilizes the comparative approach and also interweaves archeological insights. LM****

Wood, L. J. *A Survey of Israel's History.* Zondervan, 1986. xv/416 pp. 16 maps.

Wood first produced this volume in 1970; it has been updated since his death by D. O'Brien, apparently a nonspecialist. The volume is essentially a retelling of the biblical story with some archeological information thrown in. Even when it first appeared it was geared for the college classroom. That it is often used in seminaries is an indication that evangelicals have failed to produce a really helpful history of Israel. L**

Archeology

Aharoni, Y. *The Archaeology of the Land of Israel.* Trans. A. F. Rainey. Westminster, 1982 (Heb. orig. 1978). 364 pp. $18.95 pb.

Aharoni was one of the leading Israeli archeologists of the past generation. He helped train many who are in the field today. He was a scholar of great erudition and integrity, which brought him into conflict with the archeological establishment (particularly Y. Yadin). This book represents a kind of summary statement of his views on the archeological remains of Israel from the prehistoric period through the sixth century B.C. It is clearly written and well illustrated. MS****

Avi-Yonah, M. (ed.). *Encyclopedia of Archeological Excavations in the Holy Land.* 4 vols. Prentice-Hall, 1975–78.

This encyclopedia covers all of the significant archeological activity in Palestine up to the time of publication. The information is given alphabetically by site. It is a wonderful reference work and covers all periods of antiquity. MS*****

Atlases

Aharoni, Y., and M. Avi-Yonah. *The Macmillan Bible Atlas.* Macmillan, 1968 (rev. 1975). 183 pp. $29.95 hb.

This fine atlas was the staple of most seminary students at least until the recent outpouring of new atlases. It is historically oriented with a moderate critical bias. For the most part, the maps are associated with specific biblical events (Scripture references are included). Most of the maps are one-color. LM***

Beitzel, B. *The Moody Atlas of Bible Lands.* Moody, 1985. xviii/234 pp. $33.95 hb.

The *Moody Atlas,* like the *NIV Atlas,* focuses on both geography and history. Beitzel uses a combination of impressive photos and technically superior maps to describe the promised land and the surrounding nations. His prose descriptions are well written. LM*****

Monson, J. *Student Map Manual: Historical Geography of the Bible Lands.* Zondervan, n.d.

This unique atlas is a workbook to be used along with slides from the Wide Screen project. It may also be used as a workbook along with Monson's *Land Between*. A wonderful way to learn geography through hands-on experience. LM****

Pritchard, J. B. *The Harper Atlas of the Bible.* Harper and Row, 1987. 254 pp. $49.95 hb.

In terms of the technical presentation of maps and other information, this atlas may be the best of the several excellent atlases produced in the past decade. The atlas covers the period of time from before the biblical events to the founding of Byzantine churches. There is a wealth of interesting information presented in a graphically compelling way that will keep Bible students occupied for a long time. The viewpoint represented in the narrative of the atlas is a moderate critical approach. LM*****

Rasmussen, C. G. *NIV Atlas of the Bible.* Zondervan, 1989. 256 pp. $39.95 hb.

Rasmussen is well qualified to produce an atlas, being a student of historical geography and former dean of the Institute of Holy Land Studies in Jerusalem. His volume does not disappoint. He does an excellent job of surveying both the geography and the history of Israel and the ancient Near East. He presents his material clearly and succinctly. Among many other handy features, this volume includes a "Gazeteer" that lists all the sites mentioned in the volume along with a short description of their significance and references as to where to find the site in the atlas. LM****

Rogerson, J. *The Atlas of the Bible*. Facts on File, 1985. 237 pp. $40.00.

Another fine entry in the recent flood of contemporary Bible atlases, Rogerson's volume contains excellent photographs and maps. The distinctive trait of this volume is the amount of attention given to geography as opposed to history. Rogerson gives the reader a feel for the different regions of Israel. LM****

Wood, D. R. W. *New Bible Atlas*. Inter-Varsity, 1985.

This highly competent, brief atlas draws on the skills of such well-known scholars as D. J. Wiseman and J. J. Bimson. It covers the Old and New Testaments. It, like many other recent atlases, covers both geography and history. This atlas also has a helpful section that treats the lands outside of Israel. LM***

Translations of Ancient Near Eastern Texts

Beyerlin, W. (ed.). *Near Eastern Religious Texts Relating to the Old Testament*. OTL. Westminster, 1978. xxviii/228 pp.

This text presents English translations of selected Egyptian, Mesopotamian, Hittite, Ugaritic, and Northwest Semitic texts. The principle of selection is the religious nature of the texts and their utility for biblical studies. The translation is more vernacular than ANET, but the latter includes more texts. LM****

Coogan, M. D. *Stories from Ancient Canaan*. Westminster, 1978. 120 pp. $7.95 pb.

An excellent and readable translation of three major Ugaritic story cycles and two short Rephaim texts. While ANET presents these texts in KJV style, Coogan adopts a style similar to that of the RSV. LM****

Kovacs, M. G. *The Epic of Gilgamesh*. Stanford University Press, 1989. xxxiv/122 pp. $4.95 pb.

The Gilgamesh epic is one of the "classics" of literature from Mesopotamia and is of particular interest to students of the Bible because of its eleventh tablet, which contains a flood story. Kovacs provides a new, very readable translation, based on all of the texts known (at least as of 1988) from antiquity. There are a few nontechnical introductory remarks. LM****

Lambert, W. G. *Babylonian Wisdom Literature*. Oxford, 1960. xvi/358 pp.; 75 plates. $85.99 hb.

Lambert has amassed the major Babylonian texts that bear on the interpretation of biblical wisdom books. His translation is accurate. There are texts that relate to the Book of Job *(Ludlul bēl nēmēqi* and The Babylonian Theodicy), Proverbs, and Ecclesiastes (The Dialogue of Pessimism). MS****

Pritchard, J. B. (ed.). *Ancient Near Eastern Tests* (ANET). 3d ed. Princeton University Press, 1969. 758 pp. $76.00 hb.

This masterful translation of some of the most important Near Eastern texts has been of inestimable importance. ANET permits the nonspecialist to directly consult the primary sources of the study of ancient Near Eastern literature, history, and culture. The texts are from Mesopotamia, Egypt, Hatti, Ugarit, and some of the lesser known parts of the Near East. They span millennia and are grouped according to genre (history, law, myths, rituals, wisdom, hymns, lamentations, letters). Serious students should purchase the full version in hardcover, although an abridged version in paperback is available. The translators were the top scholars of the 1950s and 1960s. The only drawback of the volume is that the translation is in a very formal KJV style. MS*****

Simpson, W. K. (ed.). *The Literature of Ancient Egypt: An Anthology of Stories, Instructions, and Poetry.* Yale University Press, 1972. 345 pp. $13.95 pb.

This volume brings together a number of Egyptian compositions that are united by their literary pretensions. They are grouped by genre, these being generally described by the subtitle of the book. The translations are done by leading Egyptologists, who render the texts into contemporary English and provide short introductions. LM****

Winton-Thomas, D. (ed.). *Documents from Old Testament Times.* Harper Torchbooks, 1958. 302 pp.

When this book first appeared, ANET had not yet been published. Since the latter has incorporated most if not all of the texts treated in the former (and added a considerable number more), it is better to go with ANET. However, the translations, done by British and Canadian scholars, are excellent, as are the introductions and notes. There are examples from five different language groups: (1) cuneiform, (2) Egyptian, (3) Moabite, (4) Hebrew, and (5) Aramaic. LM**

Near Eastern History

Hallo, W. W., and W. K. Simpson. *The Ancient Near East: A History*. Harcourt Brace Jovanovich, 1971. 319 pp. $14.95 pb.

This well-written and erudite volume is an excellent introduction to the history of Mesopotamia and Egypt, written by two of the leading authorities on these areas. The story actually begins in the period before official history, but takes the reader through the millennia down to the dawn of the period of the New Testament. This volume, however, is not concerned to treat the Old Testament in any detail; it is a summary history of the broader Near East. LM****

Moscati, S. *The Face of the Ancient Orient*. Doubleday, 1962.

A readable, semipopular treatment of Near Eastern history and civilization from about 3000 B.C. until ca. 330 B.C. Moscati is a well known Semitics scholar and brings great competence to the task. The book, an English translation of an Italian original, is somewhat dated. SM**

Oppenheim, A. Leo. *Ancient Mesopotamia*. University of Chicago, 1977 (orig. 1964). xvi/443 pp. $15.00 pb.

This is one of the truly fascinating books written about Mesopotamia by an expert on the Near East. In a field often stifled by studies of minutiae, Oppenheim, who was a top scholar in the field, has produced an incredibly readable synthesis of the religion, literature, culture, and history of the region. The book must be read by anyone who desires to acquire an understanding of the Near Eastern background of the Bible. LM*****

Wiseman, D. J. *Peoples of Old Testament Times*. Oxford, 1973. xxi/442 pp.

This volume contains a collection of essays on the various peoples who surrounded Israel during the Old Testament period. First, they are described in their own right. Second, they are related to Israel and the Bible in terms of their influence. The volume was produced by members of the Society for Old Testament Studies and so reflects a high level of scholarship and a variety of different viewpoints on the Bible. LM****

Hebrew Helps

Dictionaries

✗ Brown, F., S. R. Driver, and C. A. Briggs. *Hebrew and English Lexicon of the Old Testament* (BDB). Hendrickson, 1979 (orig. 1907). 1200 pp. $34.95 hb.

This volume is the standard Hebrew dictionary written in English. It is based on the earlier work of Gesenius and Robinson, but is more than a mere update. It is an excellent work, but so much has happened since the early part of the century (one only needs to remember the discovery of Ugarit in 1929) that the work is obviously dated. While a new work is needed, this volume is still useful. Nouns are often listed under their verbal roots. Textual citations are given, although not always exhaustively. MS***

✗ Holladay, W. L. *A Concise Hebrew and Aramaic Lexicon of the Old Testament.* Eerdmans, 1971. 425 pp. $27.95 hb.

This dictionary is perhaps the most widely used by students in English-speaking environments. It is an abridgement of Koehler–Baumgartner and provides its user with the information necessary to render "an adequate translation of a given passage into English" (p. x). It has most of the strengths of its parent volume. It is easy to use and also transportable (a quality not found in many Hebrew dictionaries). MS****

Koehler, L., and W. Baumgartner. *Lexicon in Veteris Testamenti Libros* (KB). 3d ed. Eerdmans, 1951–53. 1138 pp. $49.50 hb.

This volume is of the same scope and level of BDB, but is to be preferred over it for two reasons. First, since it is a later work (1st ed. 1953), it was able to take into account the research of nearly half a century and incorporate the data that Ugarit yielded. Second, the entries are listed alphabetically rather than under the verbal root, making the dictionary much easier to use. Unfortunately, although available in the United States, the work is German and in the third edition even the English translations of the meanings have been removed. MS****

Biblical-Theological Dictionaries

Botterweck, G. J., and H. Ringgren. *Theological Dictionary of the Old Testament* (TDOT). Trans. J. T. Willis, G. W. Bromiley, and D. E. Green. Eerdmans, 1974– . $179.95 hb.

This dictionary presents the theological implications of certain important words in the Old Testament. Etymologies, frequency of occurrence, and context are covered. While there are dangers of overusing the results of these studies (for instance, reading every nuance of a word into a single occurrence), the book is enlightening and helpful as a supplement to a regular lexicon. This dictionary is a translation of a German original. The volumes have been slow in coming out (5 vols. between 1974 and 1990). MS***

Elwell, W. A. (ed.). *Baker Encyclopedia of the Bible*. 2 vols. Baker, 1988. 2000 pp. $79.95 hb.

This volume is directed toward the layperson and student. It provides commentary on all the books of the Bible as well as articles on theology, customs, society, the broader Near East, archeology, and more. There are few illustrations. LM****

Harris, R. L., G. L. Archer, Jr., and B. K. Waltke. *Theological Wordbook of the Old Testament*. 2 vols. Moody, 1980. 1200 pp. $49.95 hb.

These volumes are the work of a number of evangelical scholars. They cover most of the major and a number of the minor words of the Old Testament. The studies are uneven, but of generally high quality. The editors are aware of the potential pitfalls of word study as represented by Barr's arguments. For best results, the reader of this volume should understand Hebrew. MS****

Concordances

Even-Shoshan, E. *A New Concordance of the Bible*. Baker, 1989. 1242 pp. $55.00 hb.

The original of this work was published in Hebrew in 1977–80. This is certainly the most usable concordance, especially for English-speaking readers. The words, for instance, are listed alphabetically instead of by roots. However, it is still imperative to have a knowledge of Hebrew in order to use this reference work intelligently. MS****

Goodrick, E. W., and J. R. Kohlenberger, III. *The NIV Exhaustive Concordance* (NIVEC). Zondervan, 1990. xx/1853 pp.

This concordance is a major achievement and should be included in the library of everyone who uses the NIV. It is the first exhaustive concordance of the NIV and is beautifully produced for ease of use. LM*****

Mandelkern, S. *Veteris Testamenti Concordantiae.* 2 vols. Schocken, 1971. 1565 pp.

An excellent and detailed concordance of the Old Testament. It is only for those who know Hebrew, however, since it lists the words and their contexts in Hebrew. MS***

Strong, J. *Strong's Exhaustive Concordance.* Baker, 1989 (orig. 1894). 1420 pp. $15.95 pb.

This truly remarkable work is an English concordance of the entire Bible based on the Authorized Version. It includes verse references to every word, including frequently occurring particles like "a" and "the." For most nouns and verbs, Strong gives the verse and a brief portion of the context. It is an amazing piece of work for the precomputer age. Computer concordances will eventually replace it. LM***

Grammars

There are a number of basic Hebrew grammars with different strengths and weaknesses. Very few people learn Hebrew on their own, however; thus the choice of a first-year grammar is usually made by instructors. There are some intermediate and advanced grammars for those with a basic knowledge of Hebrew.

Cowley, A. E., and E. Kautzsch (eds.). *Gesenius' Hebrew Grammar* (GKC). 2d Eng. ed., based on the 28th Ger. ed. Oxford, 1910. 614 pp. $32.00 hb.

Commonly known as Gesenius–Kautzsch–Cowley (GKC) or simply Gesenius, this volume has been the standard advanced reference grammar for over a century and a half (the first German edition came out in 1813). It is frequently cited in the secondary literature. Its strength lies in its comprehensive survey of the grammar, combined with extensive textual citations that are easily accessible through the indexes. MS*****

Waltke, B. K., and M. O'Connor. *An Introduction to Biblical Hebrew Syntax.* Eisenbrauns, 1990. 765 pp. $37.50 hb.

This volume is the first significant intermediate- to advanced-level grammar published in many decades. It is magnificently done in terms of both content and production. The section on the verbal system is especially important. This volume is a must-buy for students of Hebrew. It is also a good way for ministers who have let their Hebrew slip to get back into it. MS*****

Text-Based Lexicons and Interlinears

Armstrong, T. A., D. L. Busby, and C. F. Carr. *A Reader's Hebrew-English Lexicon of the Old Testament.* 4 vols. Zondervan, 1980–88. $16.95 (ea.) hb.

The purpose of this multivolume work is to provide help for the beginning or average reader of Hebrew. It intends to cut down on the time it takes to look up words in a standard dictionary and thus increase the student's speed in reading. The work follows the canonical form of the text, listing and giving definitions (from BDB) for all words that occur less than fifty times in the Old Testament. All those occurring fifty times or more are found in an appendix. The authors are quick to point out that their work does not replace the standard dictionaries (each word listing also gives a page number from BDB for further detailed analysis), but has the limited function described above. Lazy and careless beginning exegetes may misuse the book to save time. The reader must be very careful since there are mistakes in the volume. M**

Beall, T. D., and W. A. Banks (with C. Smith in vol. 2). *Old Testament Parsing Guide.* 2 vols. Moody, 1986, 1990. 390, 299 pp. $29.95 (ea.) hb.

This work parses every verb in the Old Testament by occurrence. Helpful when the interpreter cannot identify a root, but abused by students who want to avoid learning paradigms. M**

Einspahr, B. *Index to Brown, Driver and Briggs.* Moody, 1976. $25.95 pb.

This volume is similar in conception with the Armstrong, Busby, Carr work. However, there are some differences. It does not limit itself to words that occur less than fifty times, but rather lists every citation given in BDB by text. The purpose of the volume is to help students get quickly to the right page in BDB. However, once again, the lazy student will be tempted to simply take the basic meaning provided by the index rather than going to the lexicon. A better alternative is to use the dictionary by Holladay, which is an abridgement of KB. M*

Kohlenberger, J. R., III. *The NIV Interlinear Hebrew-English Old Testament.* Zondervan, 1987. $69.95 hb.

The book is nicely presented, but basically provides a shortcut for seminary students. The author claims that the book can be used for word studies, but this presupposes a working knowledge of Hebrew and access to a Hebrew Bible and dictionary. M**

Owens, J. J. *Analytical Key to the Old Testament*. 4 vols. Baker, 1989– .

This tool provides a verse-by-verse study of the form of Hebrew words. Owens parses all forms, unlike Beall and Banks. Owens has provided a nice help for those who want to do some rapid reading of the Hebrew, but, like other works of this kind, the work can be abused by the lazy student. The typeface, while not difficult to read, is somewhat unpleasant to the eye. Three of the four volumes have been published. LM***

Miscellaneous

Kohlenberger, J. R., III. *The NIV Triglot Old Testament*. Zondervan, 1981. 1334 pp. $69.95 hb.

This large volume presents the Hebrew Masoretic Text, the Septuagint, and the New International Version in three columns. Serious scholars would need to consult critical editions of the Greek and Hebrew, but the three-column format allows the reader to compare the three versions at a glance. Nicely done, but profitable to only a very few. M**

The Canon of the Old Testament

Beckwith, R. *The Old Testament Canon of the New Testament Church*. Eerdmans, 1985. 536 pp. $35.00 hb.

Beckwith's book is the most significant contribution on canon in a century. His purpose is to describe the canon as it existed in the first century A.D., particularly the canon of Jesus' day. He marshals strong evidence that Jesus' canon was the same as that in contemporary Protestantism. MS*****

Leiman, S. Z. *The Canonization of Hebrew Scripture: The Talmudic and Midrashic Evidence*. Archon, 1976. 234 pp. $49.50 hb.

This is an important study that is at its most original in its analysis of the Talmudic and Midrashic materials. It departs from the older view that Jamnia was the locus of canonization. It is a good book, but most of its content has been absorbed by Beckwith. S***

The Old Testament and the Computer

Hughes, J. J. *Bits, Bytes, and Biblical Studies*. Zondervan, 1987. 643 pp. $15.95 pb.

Great developments are taking place in the area of computer-assisted biblical studies. The changes are coming so quickly that it is hard to keep abreast. Hughes provides a kind of reference guide to what is available in the area of biblical and classical studies. This basic introduction is kept up to date by his newsletter, "Bits and Bytes Review." MS*****

Commentaries

One-Volume Commentaries

One-volume commentaries are commentaries on the whole Bible bound in one volume. They generally have between 1000 and 1500 pages. While commentaries on individual books are too short to provide insight into a text, such volumes are handy to have around for a quick orientation to a book or passage of Scripture. They are relatively inexpensive and are good choices for laypeople who do not want to invest in a series.

Elwell, W. A. (ed.). *Evangelical Commentary on the Bible.* Baker, 1989. 1230 pp. $39.95 hb.

This volume is written from an evangelical perspective. It provides a good, concise theological and historical analysis of all the books of the Bible. Contributors include Raymond Dillard, Royce Gruenler, Victor Hamilton, R. K. Harrison, James Hoffmeier, Elmer Martens, Douglas Moo, Stephen Noll, R. D. Patterson, Willem VanGemeren, and Herbert Wolf. LM****

Guthrie, D., and J. A. Motyer (eds.). *The Eerdmans Bible Commentary.* Eerdmans, 1970. 1310 pp. $29.95 hb.

This volume is excellent, although it is now getting a little dated. (It used to be known as *The New Bible Commentary.*) Its many contributors are consistently good. The theological perspective is conservative. It is exegetically insightful and sound. Some of the notable contributions are by Kline (Genesis), O. T. Allis (Leviticus), Millard (Jeremiah), Kidner (Isaiah), Baldwin (Ruth and Esther), Wiseman (Haggai), and Harrison (Deuteronomy). LM***

Pfeiffer, C. F., and E. F. Harrison. *The Wycliffe Bible Commentary.* Moody, 1962. xv/1525 pp. $29.95 hb.

This is a fine one-volume commentary. Its contributors span the evangelical spectrum. Note the articles by Kline (Deuteronomy and Job), Smick (Numbers), and S. Woudstra (Song of Solomon). LM**

Sets

Publishers have found that commentaries sell best in a set. There are a number of commentary sets currently in production. The following list serves two purposes. It will describe more fully and evaluate those sets that are written by one or two authors. Second, it will describe the method of other sets by multiple authors. The individual volumes found in this second group are described and evaluated in the following section, which proceeds book-by-book through the Bible. It should be noted that sets with a number of different authors are often quite variable in terms of quality. It is often best to pick and choose among commentaries rather than committing oneself to a single set of commentaries.

The Anchor Bible (AB). Eds. W. F. Albright and D. N. Freedman. Doubleday, 1960s– .

The Anchor Bible is an indispensable tool for scholars and certain ministers, but often fails in its attempt to communicate with laypersons. It usually emphasizes philology, historical background, and text, rather than theology. The volumes range in quality from excellent to horrible. MS***

The Bible Speaks Today (BST). Ed. J. A. Motyer. Inter-Varsity, 1976– .

The purpose of this set is to write on the biblical text in a way that engages the reader. In other words, its volumes can be read cover-to-cover; they are not simply reference tools. The series is readable, accurate, and relevant. LM****

Bible Student's Commentary (BSC). Zondervan, 1970s– .

This series provides English translations of commentaries published decades ago in the Dutch series *Korte Verklaring der Heilige Schrift*. Although dated, especially in technical areas, they are very insightful theologically and represent a conservative Reformed exegesis. MS***

The Broadman Bible Commentary. 12 vols. Broadman, 1969–72.

This series is a project of Southern Baptist biblical scholars and used many fine interpreters. It may be consulted in a library, but is not recommended for purchase by an individual. LM***

Calvin's Commentaries. Baker repr., 1979.

These commentaries find their origin in Calvin's sermons, but they are learned and theologically insightful. It is no wonder that Calvin is called the "prince of expositors." Calvin does comment on language occasionally, but one will have to consult a more recent commentary because of discoveries in language. He does not cover the whole Old Testament. Volumes are missing between Judges and Job. The five-volume commentary on Psalms is wonderful. Unfortunately, Calvin harmonizes Exodus to Deuteronomy. LMS*****

The Cambridge Bible Commentary (CBC). Eds. P. R. Ackroyd, A. R. C. Leaney, and J. W. Packer. Cambridge University Press, 1971–79.

This series is composed of short and readable commentaries on all the books of the Old Testament and the Apocrypha. They intend to bring the fruits of contemporary scholarship to educated laypersons. The volumes also intend to explicate the New English Bible, which is the base of the commentary. They concentrate on both historical background and theological issues. A selection of volumes includes R. E. Clements on Exodus, P. R. Ackroyd on Samuel, R. J. Coggins on Chronicles, J. D. W. Watts on the Minor Prophets, and R. N. Whybray on Proverbs. LM***

Communicator's Commentary (CC). Ed. Lloyd Ogilvie. Word, 1987– .

This energetic series is directed toward pastors and other Christian leaders in teaching positions. For the most part, the volumes meet their intended goal and are backed by solid scholarship. They are also very readable. LM****

The Daily Study Bible (DSB). Ed. J. C. L. Gibson. Westminster, 1981– .

The DSB is the Old Testament counterpart to Barclay's New Testament commentaries. The name derives from the fact that the commentators have divided the text (RSV) into portions that can be read in a single day's devotional. The commentary is directed toward the layperson and encourages an expositional and theological reading of the text. LM****

The Expositor's Bible Commentary. Ed. F. E. Gaebelein. Zondervan, 1979– .

This is a multivolume set, but each volume contains comments on a number of biblical books and is authored by different scholars. The authors come from a general evangelical background and articulate a predominantly premillennial perspective. The series is geared for preachers, teachers, and students. There are six volumes on the Old Testament; not all of them are out yet. The scholars are for the most part quite capable in historical-grammatical exegesis. LM****

Forms of Old Testament Literature (FOTL). Eds. R. Knierim and G. M. Tucker. Eerdmans, 1981– .

When completed, this series will have twenty-four volumes. There are just a few out at present, but they represent the highly technical character of the series as a whole. The title of the series indicates its focus on a form-critical approach to the text. Judged in the light of their purpose, these are excellent commentaries. Scholars will find these books invaluable. S****

Hermeneia. Eds. F. C. Cross, et al. Fortress, 1970s– .

A number of the volumes in this series are translations of original German works, although there are some English contributions. The quality of the series is high. It intends to deliver the best of historical and critical scholarship, and usually succeeds. There are some classic works in this series. S*****

The International Critical Commentary (ICC). T. and T. Clark, turn of the century.

These are highly technical studies of philology and text. They are best used by specialists and retain their value in spite of their age. A new series is presently being written. S***

International Theological Commentary (ITC). Eerdmans, 1980s, incomplete.

This is a series of short commentaries written from a third world perspective. The purpose is to both shake off some of the assumptions of Western readers and connect the text with contemporary issues. Often provides interesting insight into the Bible. At other times, however, these volumes are scarcely distinguishable from traditional commentaries. LM**

Interpretation (Interp). Ed. J. L. Mays. John Knox, 1982– .

This series bridges the gap between scholarly investigation and contemporary relevance. Moderately critical, the series is readable and interesting. LM****

The Interpreter's Bible (IB). Ed. G. A. Buttrick. Abingdon, 1950s.

This is a cross between a set and individual book commentaries. The Old Testament is covered in six volumes. The commentary has two sections: a more technical exegetical section and an expository section. The viewpoint of the series is a moderate historical criticism typical of the 1950s. LM**

JPS Torah Commentary. Ed. N. Sarna. Jewish Publication Society, 1989– .

The series, as the title indicates, will cover only the first five books of the Hebrew Bible. The commentary prints the Hebrew text and gives copious comments on philology, history of research (with very interesting comments from rabbinic material), and theology. The content and the production of the volumes are first-rate. MS*****

Keil-Delitzsch. Eerdmans, latter half of the nineteenth century.

C. F. Keil and F. Delitzsch were orthodox Lutheran Old Testament scholars from Germany in the latter half of the nineteenth century. Their expositions, although dated, are solid and competent. They often give helpful theological commentary as well. This set is fairly inexpensive and makes a good backbone to a minister's library. LM****

Knox Preaching Guides. Ed. J. H. Hayes. John Knox, recent and still being produced.

These short paperbacks offer assistance to ministers as they prepare to preach. A number of notable contributors, including W. Brueggemann, J. J. Collins, W. Roth, E. Achtemeier, and J. G. Gammie. Moderately critical for the most part. M***

The Layman's Bible Commentary. Westminster/John Knox, about thirty years old.

Short, concise commentaries written for the layperson by critical scholars of the past generation. LM**

Leupold's Commentaries. Baker, 1942–71.

Leupold was a conservative Lutheran who wrote on many Old Testament books (Genesis, Psalms, Ecclesiastes, Isaiah, Daniel, and Zechariah). Leupold's work has value, but he tends to write more like a systematic theologian than a biblical exegete. LM**

New Century Bible (NCB). OT ed. R. E. Clements. Eerdmans, 1960s– .

The New Century Bible is a predominantly British project based on the Revised Standard Version. Many of the volumes seem restricted by the format. As a series, it is weak. There are, however, some very fine volumes. The volumes range from moderately critical to heavily critical. LM**

The New International Commentary on the Old Testament (NICOT). Ed. R. K. Harrison. Eerdmans, 1970s– .

This series was originally begun in the 1950s under E. J. Young's editorship, but was stalled after the editor produced his three-volume Isaiah commentary. Young's commentary has since been removed. The series is evangelical and scholarly, but written in a way that laypeople can understand. Technical issues as well as theological commentary are found in these commentaries. MS****

Old Testament Library (OTL). Eds. P. Ackroyd, et al. Westminster, 1960s– .

This is a distinguished collection of commentaries written in the critical tradition. Many, but not all, are translations of earlier German works. OTL includes, besides the commentaries, Eichrodt's *Theology,* Beyerlin's study of related ancient Near Eastern texts, and Soggin's history. MS***

Old Testament Message (OTM). Eds. C. Stuhlmueller and M. McNamara. Michael Glazier, 1980s– .

OTM is planned to be a twenty-three-volume set, geared for laypeople. While each volume is written by a Catholic scholar, it is hoped that the appeal will be much broader. The method is moderately critical with a premium on clarity, theology, and relevance. LM***

Text and Interpretation (TI). Ed. A. S. van der Woude. Eerdmans, 1987– .

The volumes in the series are short, semischolarly, and attempt to be relevant to contemporary society. Most of the volumes produced thus far have been fairly disappointing. LM**

Torch Bible Commentaries (TBC). Eds. J. Marsh, A. Richardson, and R. Gregor Smith. SCM, 1950–73.

This series is very similar in intent, scope, and approach to the Cambridge Bible Commentaries. The contributors were asked to make the results of modern scholarship accessible to educated laypeople within the church. Two notable contributions include J. H. Eaton on Psalms and C. R. North on Isaiah 40–55. The commentary is based on the Authorized Version. LM***

Tyndale Old Testament Commentaries (TOTC). Ed. D. J. Wiseman. Inter-Varsity, 1960s– .

These commentaries are authored by respected English, South African, Australian, Irish, and American evangelical scholars. They are in the main directed toward a nonspecialist audience. They emphasize exegesis. They are brief, but usually informative. LM****

Word Biblical Commentary (WBC). Ed. J. D. W. Watts (OT). Word, late 1970s– .

These commentaries are written by evangelicals who are identified in the preface as those who are committed "to Scripture as divine revelation, and to the truth and power of the Christian gospel." This definition allows for the wide-ranging approaches to the Bible that are found in the series. Not everyone will be satisfied that a given commentary is evangelical in the sense that they know it, although most clearly are. These commentaries are very learned, and provide their own translation with philological, textual, and literary notes. Theological message is also treated, but with few exceptions these theological comments rarely bridge the gap to the New Testament. MS****

Wycliffe Exegetical Commentary (WEC). Ed. K. Barker. Moody, 1988– .

This is the newest series on the scene. Moises Silva's commentary on Philippians and R. K. Harrison's on Numbers are the only ones to appear. On the basis of the names writing for the Old Testament side, this is a series to watch.

Individual Commentaries
Genesis

Aalders, G. C. *Genesis.* BSC. 2 vols. Zondervan, 1981. 311, 228 pp. $29.95 (set) hb.

This is an English translation of a commentary originally published in Dutch in 1949. Although somewhat dated, Aalders' work retains its value as a theological commentary. Writing from within the Reformed tradition, Aalders shows great exegetical skill and theological insight. MS***

Atkinson, D. *The Message of Genesis 1–11.* BST. Inter-Varsity, 1990. 190 pp. $12.95 pb.

A brief, expository, and devotional reading of the first part of the Book of Genesis. Atkinson is insightful and knowledgeable. LM****

Baldwin, J. G. *The Message of Genesis 12–50.* BST. Inter-Varsity, 1986. 224 pp. $9.95 pb.

Baldwin writes in a popular style, yet there is no doubt that considerable scholarly research stands behind her commentary. Her approach to Genesis 12–50 is traditional, yet not stodgy. LM***

Boice, J. M. *Genesis.* 3 vols. Zondervan, 1982–87. 366, 383, 366 pp. $14.95 (ea.) pb.

Boice, a popular Presbyterian preacher, expectedly puts a heavy emphasis on the application of the text. Unfortunately, his treatment of Old Testament narrative tends to be highly moralistic in ways which the text does not intend. LM**

Briscoe, S. *Genesis*. CC. Word, 1987. 414 pp. $19.99 hb.

Briscoe does a good job navigating the choppy waters of the difficult interpretive issues of Genesis. Not that he is always right, but he exercises fairly sensible judgment. The volume, in keeping with the purpose of the commentary, is sermonic and anecdotal, not exegetical or biblical-theological. However, what it does, it does well. LM***

Brueggemann, W. *Genesis*. Interp. John Knox, 1982. viii/384 pp. $23.95 hb.

Brueggemann, although a moderately critical scholar, is always stimulating and insightful. His commentary concentrates on the final form of the text and focuses principally on the theology of the book. LM****

Candlish, R. S. *Studies in Genesis*. Kregel, 1979 (orig. 1869). viii/843 pp. $24.95 hb.

Candlish was a prominent professor and pastor in Scotland in the middle of the last century. His comments are theological and homiletical. This is not a full commentary and is somewhat obsolete. M**

Cassuto, U. *Commentary on Genesis*. Trans. I. Abrahams. 2 vols. Magnes, 1964. xiv/386 pp. $36.95 hb.; xviii/323 pp. $40.25 hb.

This is an excellent, but expensive, commentary on the first thirteen chapters of Genesis. Cassuto, a conservative Jewish writer, died unexpectedly before the book was completed. He is a brilliant philologist and literary scholar. He, interestingly, goes against the scholarly tide and rejects the Documentary Hypothesis. S***

Coats, G. W. *Genesis with an Introduction to Narrative Literature*. FOTL. Eerdmans, 1983. xiii/322 pp. $24.95 pb.

Definitely one of the best volumes in the series thus far, this commentary nonetheless is difficult to wade through due to its focus on form-critical issues. Coats is most helpful when he deals with narrative issues from a literary standpoint. He is least help-ful when he spends time analyzing the sources of the narrative rather than concentrating on the final form of the text. S***

Davidson, R. *Genesis 1–11*. CBC. Cambridge, 1973. x/118 pp. $9.95 pb.

This brief commentary presents a critical perspective on the first chapters of Genesis to an educated popular-level audience. The introduction presents a source-critical approach to the question of composition and deals with myth and the stories of Genesis. LM**

Gibson, J. C. L. *Genesis*. DSB. 2 vols. Westminster, 1981. ix/214 pp. $12.95 hb./$6.95 pb.; ix/322 pp. $7.95 pb.

In keeping with the nature of the series, Gibson writes in a popular vein. He helpfully opens up the text for lay under-standing, showing the relevance of Genesis for the Christian. He is less helpful when he describes the composition of the book along the lines of older source criticism. LM***

Gowan, D. E. *Genesis 1–11*. ITC. Eerdmans, 1988. ix/125 pp. $10.95 pb.

A short theological study of the first eleven chapters of the Bible. While there is considerable theological reflection, the book also displays a fair share of typical critical assumptions. Gowan's treatment of the relationship between the theology and history of Genesis is quite superficial and will not satisfy many. While many of the commentaries in this series come from a third world perspective, this one does not. It also fails to interact with contemporary social and political issues to the extent of many of the other volumes. LM**

Herbert, A. S. *Genesis 12–50.* TBC. SCM, 1962. 160 pp.

Herbert assumes the literary introduction of Richardson. He believes that the patriarchal period began in 1650 B.C., a view not widely held today by liberal or conservative scholars. He sees the uniqueness of Israelite religion not in monotheism but in divine-human personal relationships. LM**

Kidner, D. *Genesis.* TOTC. Inter-Varsity, 1967. 224 pp. $14.95 hb./$8.95 pb.

This is an excellent commentary within the parameters of the series. Since it is so brief, it cannot hope to fully comment on the text. It is noticeably lacking (by design) substantial philological notes. It is written from a solidly conservative standpoint. This is a good starter commentary for the layperson. LM***

Maher, M. *Genesis.* OTM. Michael Glazier, 1982. 279 pp. $14.95 pb.

The volume may have some value in its theological commentary. It presents the rather naive critical view that Genesis is a "statement of religious truths" rather than history. Maher accepts the now dated Documentary Hypothesis, although he notes challenges to it in passing. LM**

Pink, A. W. *Gleanings in Genesis.* Moody, 1922. 408 pp. $12.95 pb.

Pink is not a biblical scholar and presents a rather rigid and dogmatic approach to the text of Genesis. The book has its place, but should not be confused with a commentary. LM*

Rad, G. von. *Genesis*. OTL. Westminster, 1972. 440 pp. $17.95 hb.

An insightful, but critical, commentary on Genesis. Von Rad is sensitive to theology and literature. He is not known for his work on the Hebrew language. He argues for the Hexateuch and delineates sources. S***

Richardson, A. *Genesis 1–11*. TBC. SCM, 1953. 134 pp.

Richardson gives a brief exposition of source criticism, although aware that the traditional sources contain older material. He treats the main stories of the first few chapters of Genesis as parables, avoiding the label "myth" because the lay mind equates that term with falsity. LM**

Ross, Allen P. *Creation and Blessing: A Guide to the Study and Exposition of Genesis*. Baker, 1988. 744 pp. $29.95 hb.

The book opens with a short introduction to the whole book, stating the author's method of approach to Genesis. Ross presents an evangelical alternative to the documentary approach. The bulk of his treatment, however, is more like a running exposition with an emphasis on theology. As such it is often insightful and helpful. A good book, especially for pastors preaching through the Book of Genesis. LM****

Sarna, N. M. *Understanding Genesis: The Heritage of Biblical Israel*. Schocken, 1966. 245 pp. $8.95 pb.

This readable commentary is written from a pious Jewish perspective that takes into account a moderate historical-critical approach and attempts to make it meaningful and relevant to an educated lay audience. Sarna believes that God can work through four sources (JEDP) as well as a unified book and further argues that historical criticism supports rather than denies faith. Short, but readable, with an emphasis on interpretation and comparative studies. MS***

Sarna, N. M. *Genesis.* JPS Torah Commentary. Jewish Publication Society, 1989. xxi/414 pp. $49.95 hb.

This commentary is considerably more academic in approach than the one published in 1966. It studies the text in a verse-by-verse, virtually word-by-word manner. Although Sarna recognizes the composite nature of Genesis, he treats the book as a whole in the commentary. His emphasis, although he deals with other aspects of the text, is on Near Eastern background and Jewish tradition. MS****

Skinner, J. *A Critical and Exegetical Commentary on Genesis.* ICC. T. and T. Clark, 1910. lxvi/552 pp. $29.95 hb.

This volume represents the best of turn-of-the-century critical thought. Skinner does a detailed source analysis of the book along the lines of the Documentary Hypothesis. This is an extremely detailed commentary. Helpful grammatical information may be found here. The book is in small print, however, and is often hard to read. Not recommended for the layperson or pastor. S**

Speiser, E. A. *Genesis.* AB. Doubleday, 1964. lxxiv/379 pp. $18.00 hb.

Speiser takes a fairly classical critical approach to the Book of Genesis in terms of the delineation of sources. The introduction separates P, J, and E sources (the order in which they make their appearance in the book) and then discusses the residue. Speiser is of some help in matters of language, since he was one of the preeminent Semitic linguists of his day. This commentary is a must-buy for the scholar, but probably of little use to anyone else. S**

Wenham, G. J. *Genesis 1–15*. WBC. Word, 1987. liii/353 pp. $24.95 hb.

Wenham is one of the finest evangelical commentators today. His commentary on Genesis shows his high level of scholarship and his exegetical sensitivity. He represents a conservative approach to Genesis, but this does not involve a complete rejection of a source theory to the book. He will soon publish a second volume that will complete his commentary on Genesis. LM*****

Westermann, C. *Genesis*. 3 vols. Augsburg, 1984–86. xii/636, 604, 269 pp. $39.95 (ea.) hb.

These three volumes were originally published in German between 1974 and 1982. This commentary is a full-orbed approach that takes into account text, form, setting, interpretation, purpose, and thrust. It also provides excellent bibliographies for each section and synthesizes previous research. It claims to be the first major commentary on Genesis in decades, and is from a moderately critical stance. MS****

Westermann, C. *Genesis*. TI. Eerdmans, 1987. xiii/338 pp. $16.95 pb.

This is a shortened form of Westermann's three-volume work. Westermann omits much of his technical analysis for this more popularly oriented study. M****

Youngblood, R. *The Book of Genesis: An Introductory Commentary.* Baker, 1991. 295 pp. $17.95 pb.

This volume is a reworking of two volumes which Youngblood published in 1976 and 1980. The focus is on the book's teaching, not on philology or form. The introduction, which deals with questions of authorship and date among other issues, is adequate for the volume which is directed toward laypeople. The writing style is engaging and clear. LM***

Exodus

Burns, R. J. *Exodus, Leviticus, Numbers.* OTM. Michael Glazier, 1983. 298 pp. $15.95 hb./$9.95 pb.

The author takes a traditional literary-critical approach to these three Pentateuchal books. She asserts that Exodus "must be read as a religious creed and not as a historical chronicle" (p. 19). She does not treat every chapter of all three books, and Leviticus and Numbers get less attention than Exodus. LM**

Cassuto, U. *Commentary on Exodus.* Trans. I. Abrahams. Magnes, 1967. xvi/509 pp. $40.25 hb.

Cassuto rejects the Documentary Hypothesis and explains the existing text. He is sensitive to the literary artistry of Exodus and brilliant in his philological analysis. See also comments under his commentary on Genesis. S***

Childs, B. S. *The Book of Exodus.* OTL. Westminster, 1974. xxv/659 pp. $27.95 hb.

This is easily the best commentary on Exodus and one of the best on any biblical book. Childs divides his commentary into different sections, including textual criticism and philology, critical methods, Old Testament context, New Testament context, and history of interpretation. Although representing a critical perspective, this volume is valuable to evangelical ministers. MS*****

Cole, R. Alan. *Exodus.* TOTC. Inter-Varsity, 1973. 239 pp. $14.95 hb/$8.95 pb.

As is the case with all the volumes in this series, this is a book with all the inherent disadvantages of a short commentary. There is not much on matters of general introduction or interaction with source criticism, but there is an excellent theological introduction. It is definitely worth the price. LM***

Dunnam, M. D. *Exodus.* CC. Word, 1987. 395 pp. $19.99 hb.

As with most of the volumes in this series, this one is heavier on anecdotes and sermonic application than a serious study of the book's content. Of course, such a study can be a useful supplement to other commentaries, especially for ministers as they seek to bridge the gap between the ancient world and that of a modern congregation. LM***

✗   Durham, J. I. *Exodus.* WBC. Word, 1987. xxxiv/516 pp. $25.95 hb.

The strength of this commentary is its focus on the theology of the text. Its weakness is its casual attitude toward the historicity of Exodus. Durham identifies the heart of the book's message as the presence of God with his people. MS****

Ellison, H. L. *Exodus.* DSB. Westminster, 1982. 203 pp. $12.95 hb./$7.95 pb.

Ellison does a good job explaining the text to the modern lay reader. He is insightful, but the commentary is too brief. The introduction is short even for the series, and makes only passing reference to the critical problems of history. Ellison emphasizes theology and is committed to a New Testament approach after studying the text in its Old Testament context. LM**

Gispen, W. H. *Exodus.* BSC. Zondervan, 1982. 335 pp. $19.95 hb.

Gispen's work was originally published in Dutch in 1951. It is full of helpful exegetical and theological insights from a Reformed perspective. MS***

Hyatt, J. B. *Exodus.* NCB. Eerdmans, 1971. 351 pp. $12.95 pb.

Hyatt takes a critical approach to the Book of Exodus. His comments are brief and sketchy. There is very little theological or literary exposition. The book, however, has a series of excurses on various topics of interest, such as the origin of Mosaic Yahwism and the passover. Worthwhile only if one is interested in a critical perspective on an issue. S**

Noth, M. *Exodus.* OTL. Westminster, 1962. 283 pp. $17.95 hb.

Noth is one of the most important German critical scholars of this century. He concentrates on historical and literary issues from a critical perspective. This is an important piece of scholarship, but will not help the pastor or layperson. S***

Leviticus

Bonar, A. A. *A Commentary on Leviticus.* Banner of Truth, 1978 (orig. 1846). 529 pp. $21.40 hb.

This commentary is rightly esteemed by many evangelical students of the Bible. Its strength lies in its typological approach to Leviticus. It looks at the book through the prism of the Book of Hebrews. While some of his correspondences will not appeal to modern readers, Bonar does restrain himself by looking for "obvious resemblance" between Old Testament ritual and New Testament reality. LM***

Demarest, G. W. *Leviticus.* CC. Word, 1990. 286 pp. $19.99 hb.

Demarest confesses that he struggled to come to grips with the meaning and significance of this biblical book. The results are often satisfying, and he provides a helpful introduction to the relevance of the book especially geared to those who are teaching or preaching from Leviticus. It should be supplemented by a more academic volume for serious study. LM***

Harrison, R. K. *Leviticus.* TOTC. Inter-Varsity, 1980. 252 pp. $8.95 pb.

Harrison is one of the most competent Old Testament evangelical scholars today. The commentary is too short to compete with Wenham's volume, but still well worth having. LM****

Kellogg, S. H. *Studies in Leviticus.* Kregel, 1988 (orig. 1891). 576 pp. $22.95 hb./$16.95 pb.

This commentary bears many similarities to the commentary by Bonar. Leviticus lends itself to the kind of typological studies that fascinated biblical students of that day. It would be beneficial to have a commentary that combines the careful scholarship of the present day with the theological sensitivity of Bonar and Kellogg. Wenham comes closest. LM**

Knight, G. A. F. *Leviticus*. DSB. Westminster, 1981. 173 pp. $12.95 hb./$6.95 pb.

While moderately critical in his approach to the book, Knight provides a helpful exposition of what the book means in its Old Testament context and devotes considerable attention to its relevance for the Christian. One of the better volumes of the series. LM****

Levine, B. A. *Leviticus*. JPS Torah Commentary. Jewish Publication Society, 1989. xlvi/284 pp. $49.95 hb.

Levine writes with the educated layperson in mind. His writing style is accessible, while he treats topics that the scholar would be interested in. Levine is one of the true experts on Leviticus and presents a stimulating and important study of the book within its context in the ancient world. He is also theologically sensitive. MS****

Noordtzij, A. *Leviticus*. BSC. Zondervan, 1982. xi/280 pp. $15.95 hb.

This commentary is a translation of a Dutch original and presents a basic evangelical approach to the text, although Noordtzij believes that some of the laws are post-Mosaic. He is theologically sensitive and responsible. MS****

Porter, J. R. *Leviticus*. CBC. Cambridge, 1976. x/232 pp. $11.95 pb.

This is a brief but well written study of a difficult biblical book. Porter presents a clearly critical position on the book. He shows sensitivity to theological issues and the question of the relevance of the book for today. LM***

Snaith, N. H. *Leviticus and Numbers*. NCB. Eerdmans, 1967. xii/352 pp. $8.95 pb.

Snaith is a competent Hebraist, so it is not surprising that the strength of this volume is in the areas of textual criticism and philology. The commentary suffers from the restraints of the series. It is really a brief, sketchy commentary on the RSV. Although there is little theological reflection, the text is clearly written from a critical perspective. S**

Wenham, G. J. *The Book of Leviticus*. NICOT. Eerdmans, 1979. xiii/362 pp. $29.95 hb.

Wenham has provided a fascinating and extremely helpful discussion of what most Christians regard as a drab book. He does an excellent job in explaining the holiness laws and their function in ancient Israel. It is a well written commentary. MS*****

Numbers

Budd, P. J. *Numbers*. WBC. Word, 1984. xxxii/409 pp. $25.00 hb.

This is a well researched and thought-out commentary. It employs a source-critical methodology in a way that will offend some evangelicals. It is weak in the area of biblical theology. S**

Gray, G. B. *Numbers*. ICC. T. and T. Clark, 1903. lii/489 pp. $29.95 hb.

This commentary is highly technical, very critical, and somewhat dated. Its valuable points have been incorporated into other, more recent commentaries. S**

Harrison, R. K. *Numbers*. WEC. Moody, 1990. xvi/452 pp. $25.95.

This is the first Old Testament volume to appear in Moody's new series. This particular volume takes a verse-by-verse approach (as opposed to Silva's Philippians commentary in the same series). It emphasizes exegesis and exposition, in this case with a strong focus on history and Near Eastern background, although there are many insightful theological comments as well. Harrison provides a competent defense of a traditionally orthodox approach to the book. However, he often addresses side issues rather than the real heart of the passage. MS***

Maarsingh, B. *Numbers*. TI. Eerdmans, 1987. vi/122 pp. $7.95 pb.

This commentary is very brief and not particularly satisfying. Money is better spent on larger commentaries. M*

Milgrom, J. *Numbers*. JPS Torah Commentary. Jewish Publication Society, 1990. lxi/520 pp. $49.95.

This commentary is a masterpiece of erudition. The seventy-seven excurses are themselves worth the money. Milgrom gives the reader a careful study of the details and general message of the book. He is concerned to share the insights of medieval Jewish commentators, which are inaccessible to those who do not read postbiblical Hebrew. MS*****

Noordtzij, A. *Numbers*. BSC. Zondervan, 1983. ix/304 pp. $19.95 hb.

Originally published in Dutch in 1953, this commentary is particularly helpful in the area of theology. Other commentaries would be more helpful in terms of the legal portions of Numbers. MS***

Philip, J. *Numbers*. CC. Word, 1987. 364 pp. $20.00 hb.

Philip is a prominent Scottish church leader who writes in an engaging style about the theology and significance of this rather neglected book. The commentary is backed by solid scholarship. Philip writes anecdotally with the pastor primarily in mind. LM****

Riggans, W. *Numbers*. DSB. Westminster, 1983. 252 pp. $14.95 hb./$7.95 pb.

Riggans does a good job relating the ancient biblical world to the modern one laypeople readily understand. He emphasizes the theological and practical aspects of the book. In keeping with the purpose of the series, he does not get much into introductory issues. LM***

Snaith, N. H. *Leviticus and Numbers*. NCB. Eerdmans, 1967.

See under Leviticus.

Wenham, G. J. *Numbers*. TOTC. Inter-Varsity, 1981. 240 pp. $14.95 hb./$8.95 pb.

Wenham does a wonderful job making this often neglected book come alive theologically. It is only to be lamented that the confines of the series have restricted the length of this commentary. Highly recommended for students, pastors, and scholars. LM****

Deuteronomy

Clifford, R. *Deuteronomy with Excursus on Covenant and Law.* OTM. Michael Glazier, 1982. 193 pp. $12.95 hb./$9.95 pb.

Clifford, well-known for his scholarly articles, dates the Book of Deuteronomy late and gives a two-hundred-year period of composition. He identifies the genre of the book as "speech modelled on covenant formulary" (p. 3). The excursus is short but covers an important topic. Readable. LM***

Craigie, P. C. *The Book of Deuteronomy.* NICOT. Eerdmans, 1976. 424 pp. $24.95 hb.

Craigie is among the best of recent evangelical interpreters. His work on Deuteronomy is no exception to the high quality of his work. He is an astute theologian and philologist. He adopts a firmly evangelical approach to the Book of Deuteronomy, evident in his insistence on the essential unity of the book based on the treaty analogy. LM****

Cunliffe-Jones, G. *Deuteronomy.* TBC. SCM, 1951. 191 pp.

The author attempts to bring home the complex issues surrounding the critical study of the book to laypeople. He asserts that since the book was written before Jesus Christ, "we must expect to find in it defects and distortions as well as true affirmations of faith." LM**

Driver, S. R. *A Critical and Exegetical Commentary on Deuteronomy*. ICC. T. and T. Clark, 1895. xcv/434 pp. $29.95 hb.

In many ways, this commentary is outdated. It retains its value because of Driver's ability as a philologist. Represents a turn-of-the-century critical view. S**

Miller, P. D., Jr. *Deuteronomy*. Interp. John Knox, 1990. xv/253 pp. $21.95 hb.

Miller is theologically concerned and sensitive to literary form in this helpful and well-written study. His appproach is moderately critical, and his writing style is engaging. He deals with academic questions and cites previous studies, but his primary concern is with the meaning of the canonical text. M****

Maxwell, J. C. *Deuteronomy*. CC. Word, 1987. 351 pp. $19.99 hb.

The focus of this commentary is the relevance of Deuteronomy today. Of course, such a concern is admirable, but in this case sometimes results in stretching the text's original purpose. Nonetheless, Maxwell's comments are usually on the mark. LM***

Mayes, A. D. H. *Deuteronomy*. NCB. Eerdmans, 1979. 416 pp. $8.95 pb.

Shares some of the shortcomings of the series in that it comments on the RSV and is too brief. It is among the best in the series, however. Comes from a critical perspective. LM***

Payne, D. F. *Deuteronomy*. DSB. Westminster, 1985. 197 pp. $14.95 hb./ $7.95 pb.

Payne writes clearly and nontechnically in this highly informative commentary. He divides the book into over eighty sections and gives each a catchy title. This commentary remains open to the question of date. Nonetheless, it acknowledges that the book's message is especially relevent to times of political disaster. Payne examines Deuteronomy as a book of law, as a sermon, and as history. LM****

Rad, J. von. *Deuteronomy*. OTL. Westminster, 1966. 211 pp. $15.95 hb.

Von Rad was one of the chief figures in Old Testament studies in the 1950s and beyond. He helped shape the method of study for the field during that time. This brief (especially considering the central importance of Deuteronomy to von Rad's research) commentary illustrates his approach and many of his most significant conclusions. His approach combines source, form, and redaction criticism. He concludes that while the final form of Deuteronomy is associated with Josiah's reform, the book was the product of northern Levites. S***

Ridderbos, J. *Deuteronomy*. BSC. Zondervan, 1984 (orig. 1950/51). 336 pp. $19.95 hb.

Ridderbos, one of the best Dutch Old Testament scholars of the previous generation, has contributed a formidable conservative defense against critical theories of this book. He defends essential Mosaic authorship, while also recognizing the work of a later redactor. In the commentary proper, Ridderbos is theologically sensitive and exegetically insightful. He relates this Old Testament book to our New Testament situation. ML****

Thompson, J. A. *Deuteronomy.* TOTC. Inter-Varsity, 1974. 320 pp. $14.95 hb./$8.95 pb.

Although brief, this commentary is stimulating and full of helpful information. Thompson makes good use of the treaty analogy to Deuteronomy. He deals with many of the critical issues of the book from an evangelical perspective. Contains a thoughtful essay on the difficult question of the date of the book. Some good discussion of the theology of the book. LM****

Joshua

Auld, A. G. *Joshua, Judges, and Ruth.* DSB. Westminster, 1984. 290 pp. $15.95 hb./$6.95 pb.

A short, but insightful and extremely readable exposition. In a brief introduction, Auld expresses a skeptical view concerning historicity, but his theological sensitivities redeem the volume. LM****

Boling, R. G., and G. E. Wright. *Joshua.* AB. Doubleday, 1982. xvii/580 pp. $22.00 hb.

Wright's untimely death prevented his full participation in this project; most of the work is that of his well-known student Boling (who also did the Judges commentary for this series). The commentary is critical in its approach to the text and theology of Joshua. The history and archeology of Israel are emphasized. MS**

Butler, T. *Joshua.* WBC. Word, 1983. xliii/304 pp. $22.95 hb.

A well-researched and thought-through commentary. Full of philological, textual, and exegetical information and insight. An evangelical, but not traditional, viewpoint on the book. MS***

Davis, D. R. *No Falling Words: Expositions of the Book of Joshua*. Baker, 1988. 204 pp. $9.95 pb.

This is a devotional commentary full of anecdotes and personal dialogue between the author and the reader. It is helpful for the layperson and pastor, but the serious student will need to supplement it with a more substantial commentary. LM**

Goslinga, C. J. *Joshua, Judges, Ruth*. BSC. Zondervan, 1986. 558 pp. $20.95 hb.

This commentary was translated from a Dutch original that dates from the late 1920s and early 1930s. Although it may not take into account the most recent scholarship, it is an excellent commentary from an evangelical-Reformed standpoint. Strong on theology. MS***

Gray, J. *Joshua, Judges and Ruth*. NCB. Eerdmans, 1967 (rev. 1986). 427 pp. $12.95 pb.

Follows Noth in attributing both Joshua and Judges to the Deuteronomist (and assumes a seventh-century date for Deuteronomy). Gray believes that Joshua is of limited value as a historical work. He believes that Judges is a more sober account of history. S*

Hamlin, E. J. *Joshua: Inheriting the Land*. ITC. Eerdmans, 1983. xxiii/207 pp. $10.95 pb.

This is an engagingly written exposition of Joshua that looks at the book as a continuation of the Exodus pattern. Hamlin examines the conquest in the light of the theme of the liberation of the oppressed and asks how the text is relevant for today. The book imbibes of a moderate historical criticism to make its point. M***

Hoppe, L. *Joshua, Judges*. OTM. Michael Glazier, 1982. $12.95 hb./$8.95 pb.

A popularly oriented theological study of the final form of the text. Hoppe helpfully orients his readers to the concept of the Deuteronomic history. He is less successful in dealing with the important theological concept of holy war. LM**

Huffman, J. A., Jr. Joshua. CC. Word, 1986. 282 pp. $19.99 hb.

Huffman follows the format of the series to a tee. He effectively relates the book to modern lay concerns. By use of anecdote and illustration, Huffman stimulates thinking about how to communicate the book's message. However, it is important to use this commentary with a more content-oriented one at hand. LM***

Miller, J. M., and G. M. Tucker. *The Book of Joshua*. CBC. Cambridge, 1974. x/206 pp. $9.95 pb.

The authors give a careful description of the literary composition of the book from a critical perspective. They concentrate on the Deuteronomistic redaction, which they think is the strongest voice in the book. They exaggerate supposed contradictions in the book, and use archeology to inform the Bible. LM**

Schaeffer, F. A. *Joshua and the Flow of Biblical History*. Inter-Varsity, 1975. 215 pp. $7.95 pb.

Schaeffer was a popular apologist of the faith, not a biblical scholar, but his reflections on the Book of Joshua are insightful and interesting. This volume will need to be supplemented by others for serious study. L**

Soggin, J. *Joshua*. OTL. Westminster, 1972. xvii/245 pp.

Soggin, an Italian scholar writing in the German tradition, emphasizes historical and archeological studies. Not much theological comment. S**

Woudstra, M. *The Book of Joshua*. NICOT. Eerdmans, 1981. xiv/396 pp. $24.95 hb.

Woudstra gives a very good exegetical analysis of the book. He also has an excellent biblical theological sense. There are some good literary observations, but much more could be done in this area. LM***

Judges

Auld, A. G. *Joshua, Judges, and Ruth*. DSB. Westminster, 1984.

See under Joshua.

Boling, R. G. *Judges*. AB. Doubleday, 1975. xxi/338 pp. $18.00 hb.

This volume is perhaps one of the most well-known recent commentaries on the Book of Judges. It is competently written from a critical perspective with an emphasis on history, comparative studies, and philology. Boling suggests a peasant revolt model of the conquest and believes that Israel's early social structure is similar to Greek amphictyonies. He also utilizes the covenant-treaty analogy. There is not much in the way of literary or theological reflection, as is typical of the series. MS***

Cundall, A. E., and L. Morris. *Judges and Ruth*. TOTC. Inter-Varsity, 1968. 318 pp. $14.95 hb./$8.95 pb.

Cundall's section on Judges is an adequate, but not outstanding, treatment of that book. He argues for a conservative position on the historicity of Judges and Joshua, believing the two books give complementary, and not contradictory, perspectives on the conquest. LM**

Davis, D. R. *Judges: Such a Great Salvation*. Baker, 1990. 227 pp. $11.95 pb.

This volume is the second in a series (see under Joshua). It is an anecdotal and homiletical commentary on the book. The strictures mentioned above apply here as well. This book is a little too cute. L**

Goslinga, C. J. *Joshua, Judges, Ruth*. BSC. Zondervan, 1986.

See under Joshua.

Gray, J. *Joshua, Judges and Ruth*. NCB. Eerdmans, 1967.

See under Joshua.

Hamlin, E. J. *Judges: At Risk in the Promised Land*. ITC. Eerdmans, 1990. xii/182 pp. $12.95 pb.

This volume is one of the more interesting in the series. By comparison with other contemporary cultures (particularly Chinese) and by dwelling on the theological and practical ramifications of the text ("Perspectives"), Hamlin causes the reader to look at the text in new ways. LM****

Lewis, A. H. *Judges/Ruth*. EBC. Moody, 1979. 128 pp. $5.95 pb.

Lewis writes on a popular level and in a devotional vein. He does integrate some scholarly material and uses archeological information. LM**

Martin, J. D. *The Book of Judges*. CBC. Cambridge, 1975. x/234 pp.

This commentary is a concise statement of current critical theory on the Book of Judges. Martin is historically skeptical. For instance, he connects the Samson stories with sun mythology. LM**

Moore, G. F. *A Critical and Exegetical Commentary on Judges*. ICC. T. and T. Clark, 1895. 476 pp. $29.95 hb.

Like the other volumes in this series, Moore's commentary is critical and highly technical. S**

Soggin, J. A. *Judges*. OTL. Westminster, 1981. xx/305 pp. $21.95 hb.

Once again, as in his commentary on Joshua, Soggin concentrates on critical and historical issues. He consciously avoids making theological statements. However, this is a more mature and profitable commentary than his earlier one on Joshua. S***

Ruth

Atkinson, D. *The Message of Ruth*. BST. Inter-Varsity, 1983. 128 pp. $9.95 pb.

Atkinson is an interesting writer here as he is in his Genesis 1–11 commentary. He gives some stimulating illustrations as he exposits the major themes of the book. He focuses on providence. LM****

Auld, A. G. *Joshua, Judges, and Ruth*. DSB. Westminster, 1984.

See under Joshua.

Campbell, E. F., Jr. *Ruth*. AB. Doubleday, 1975. xx/189 pp. $18.00 hb.

This is a very stimulating and well written commentary. Campbell explores many of the ancient social conventions that lie behind the text (levirate marriage, the kinsman redeemer, the removal of the sandal). He provides an early example of literary analysis. MS****

Cundall, A. E., and L. Morris. *Judges and Ruth*. TOTC. Inter-Varsity, 1968. $14.95 hb./$8.95 pb.

See under Judges. Morris, a New Testament scholar, comments on Ruth. He shows a good knowledge of the Old Testament and its background. LM**

Fuerst, W. J. *The Books of Ruth, Esther, Ecclesiastes, the Song of Songs, Lamentations*. CBC. Cambridge, 1975. x/267 pp.

These five books are grouped together since they each have a place in one of the five major Jewish festivals. Fuerst provides a helpful, although somewhat critical approach to these books. LM***

Goslinga, C. J. *Joshua, Judges, Ruth*. BSC. Zondervan, 1986.

See under Joshua.

Gray, J. *Joshua, Judges and Ruth*. NCB. Eerdmans, 1967.

See under Joshua.

✕   Hubbard, R. L., Jr. *The Book of Ruth*. NICOT. Eerdmans, 1988. xiv/317 pp. $26.95 hb.

This commentary's introduction is extensive and profitable as it discusses issues of unity, theology, canonicity, text, and more. The book as a whole demonstrates careful scholarship, a lively writing style, and balanced judgment. Hubbard pays attention to all aspects of the Book of Ruth. This commentary is one of the very best of the series. MS*****

Knight, G. A. F. *Ruth and Jonah*. TBC. SCM, 1950. 93 pp.

These two books are surprisingly treated together on the principle that they both deal with the postexilic problem of how to live with those outside of ethnic boundaries and take a tolerant stand as opposed to Ezra. LM**

Murphy, R. E. *Job, Proverbs, Ruth, Canticles, Ecclesiastes, Esther*. FOTL. Eerdmans, 1981.

See under Job.

Sasson, J. M. *Ruth: A New Translation with a Philological Commentary and a Formalist-Folklorist Interpretation.* 2d ed. JSOT, 1989 (orig. 1979). 336 pp. $19.95 pb.

This major scholarly study needs to be consulted on philological matters. Sasson shows great literary sensitivity, depending on V. Propp for formal analysis. The commentary is a repository of discussion on the book. S****

Samuel

Ackroyd, P. R. *The First Book of Samuel.* CBC. Cambridge, 1977. 238 pp. $12.95 pb. *The Second Book of Samuel.* CBC. Cambridge, 1977. xii/247 pp. $13.95 pb.

Although his expertise is in the Persian period, Ackroyd is one of the best English biblical scholars of the generation and produces a competent critical commentary on 1 Samuel. He writes clearly and for a popular audience. He is skeptical about the historicity of the book. LM***

Anderson, A. A. *2 Samuel.* WBC. Word, 1989. xl/302 pp. $24.99 hb.

This commentary is thoroughly researched and meticulously presented. Anderson does a good job presenting the critical issues of the book and also expressing his own moderately critical perspective. He does an especially good job dealing with the important text-critical problem of the book. The bibliographies are well done. A number of unfortunate typographical errors can be found. MS****

Baldwin, J. *1 and 2 Samuel.* TOTC. Inter-Varsity, 1988. 299 pp. $14.95 hb./$8.95 pb.

Baldwin's commentary is characterized by careful and up-to-date scholarship. She writes with the educated layreader in mind. In the introduction, she critiques some critical theories of composition (Wellhausen and Noth). She leaves the question up in the air, since the biblical material is not specific. The emphasis of the commentary is on exegesis and theology. LM****

✗ Brueggemann, W. *First and Second Samuel*. Interp. John Knox, 1990. x/362 pp. $24.95 hb.

Brueggemann, who produced the highly regarded Genesis commentary in this series, has produced a fascinating study of Samuel. His writing style is not just engaging but also exciting. He is a moderate critic who takes a canonical approach to the text. LM****

Chafin, K. L. *1, 2 Samuel*. CC. Word, 1989. 404 pp. $19.99 hb.

Chafin devotes more space than is typical in this series to the interpretation and explanation of the biblical text. He also uses the anecdotal style which characterizes the other volumes. He has a good grasp of the text, although (as with the series as a whole) he would benefit from a healthy dose of biblical theology. LM***

Conroy, C. *1–2 Samuel; 1–2 Kings*. OTM. Michael Glazier, 1983. 266 pp. $12.95 hb./ $8.95 pb.

Conroy has written competently on a scholarly level on Samuel before doing this commentary. He is sensitive to the book as literature. He has an excursus on David and Zion in the Old Testament, but could have developed the New Testament connections more extensively. LM***

Gordon, R. P. *1 and 2 Samuel*. Zondervan, 1988. 375 pp. $17.95 pb.

This commentary is a refreshing literary reading of Samuel. It is full of good theological insight and occasional philological and textual comments. MS****

Hertzberg, H. W. *I and II Samuel*. OTL. Westminster, 1964. 416 pp.

A good exegetical commentary from a critical perspective. Not much theological help. MS***

X   Klein, R. W. *I Samuel*. WBC. Word, 1983. xxxiii/307 pp. $22.95 hb.

This commentary is particularly helpful as a guide to the text-critical, philological, and historical issues of the Book of 1 Samuel. It should be noted that textual issues are particularly important for this book. Klein has chosen not to concentrate on literary or theological issues and this weakens the commentary. MS****

McCarter, P. Kyle, Jr., *I Samuel* and *II Samuel*. AB. Doubleday, 1980, 1984. xii/475 pp. $19.95 hb. xviii/553 pp. $22.00 hb.

McCarter is the most competent text critic to deal with Samuel, although in terms of conclusions Klein is probably better since he tends to stick with the MT more often (and this appears warranted by the evidence). McCarter, however, had access to the Dead Sea Scrolls of Samuel. Although written from a critical perspective, this commentary is well worth having. MS****

Mauchline, J. *1 and 2 Samuel.* NCB. Eerdmans, 1971. 336 pp.

Mauchline's commentary suffers from the limits of this series. It is a commentary on the RSV and too short. Of very little help. S*

Payne, D. F. *I and II Samuel.* DSB. Westminster, 1982. viii/278 pp. $12.95 hb./$7.95 pb.

Payne's style is very accessible in the tradition of DSB. He makes ancient customs understandable and emphasizes a theological exposition. He identifies the leading theme of the book as leadership—a theme that anticipates Christ. LM***

Smith, H. P. *Samuel.* ICC. T. and T. Clark, 1899. xxxix/421 pp. $29.95 hb.

Although less so than other volumes in the series, this commentary is highly technical and not easy to read. It imbibes the same optimistic critical attitude of other biblical studies at the turn of the century. Smith spends considerable time delineating sources and contradictory teachings within the book. S**

Kings

Auld, A. G. *Kings.* DSB. Westminster, 1986. ix/259 pp. $15.95 hb./$8.95 pb.

Auld gives a clear, simple exposition of the text. He emphasizes meaning and application. LM***

Cogan, M., and H. Tadmor. *II Kings.* AB. Doubleday, 1988. xxxv/371 pp. $20.00 hb.

Cogan and Tadmor are historically oriented experts in Mesopotamian studies. Thus it is not surprising that they concentrate on the Mesopotamian historical backdrop of the book. The introduction to Kings will be written when they complete the first volume. S****

✕ DeVries, S. *I Kings*. WBC. Word, 1985. lxiv/286 pp. $24.95 hb.

DeVries takes a traditional critical approach to the Book of Kings. He is heavy on source, form, and redaction criticism. These critical methods have an important function to play if used correctly. Unfortunately, they are abused here. Very little theological or exegetical insight. S**

Dilday, R. H., Jr. *1, 2 Kings*. CC. Word, 1987. 512 pp. $19.99 hb.

This is not one of the stronger volumes in the series. It would have been much better had the introduction been expanded to include an extensive discussion of the book's theological purpose and sermonic tone. As it is, the commentary tends to be moralistic. LM**

✗ Gray, J. *I and II Kings*. OTL. Westminster, 1963. 744 pp.

This has been the classic commentary on Kings for the past twenty-five years. Gray presents especially detailed work on chronology and sources from a critical perspective. There is not much theological commentary. S***

Hobbs, T. R. *2 Kings*. WBC. Word, 1985. xlviii/388 pp. $24.95.

A well-written and insightful commentary. Its helpful methodological presupposition is that 2 Kings is the work of one author. Hobbs utilizes the literary approach to great benefit. MS****

✗   Jones, G. H. *1 and 2 Kings*. NCB. 2 vols. Eerdmans, 1985. lii/666 pp. $12.95 (ea.) pb.

This two-volume commentary is one of the best in the series. In the first place, the commentary is proportionally longer than most volumes in NCB, allowing for fuller comment. Jones has a more extensive introduction and bibliography, which also increases the commentary's value. LM***

Long, B. O. *1 Kings with an Introduction to Historical Literature*. FOTL. Eerdmans, 1984. xv/265 pp. $21.95 pb.

Long provides a thoughtful study of the Book of Kings and the nature of Israelite historiographical literature from a critical theological perspective. It is particularly gratifying that he is attuned to contemporary literary theory. From an evangelical point of view, his view of the historicity of the text is low. S***

Montgomery, J. A., and J. S. Gehman. *Kings*. ICC. T. and T. Clark, 1951. xlvii/575 pp. $29.95 hb.

Montgomery's commentary was originally scheduled for publication over a decade before it appeared but was delayed by the war. Due to his death in 1949, it fell to his student, Gehman, to put the work in final form. Montgomery's contribution is extremely erudite and technical in keeping with the nature of the series. He concentrates on textual criticism, issues of composition, chronology, and the nature of historiography in the introduction. S***

Nelson, R. *First and Second Kings.* Interp. John Knox, 1987. 252 pp. $19.95 hb.

In keeping with the series, Nelson, a respected scholar on these books, concentrates on theology and literature, not history. Among other things, he emphasizes the connection with the world of Deuteronomy. He writes in a vivid and engaging style. M****

Rice, G. *I Kings: Nations under God.* ITC. Eerdmans, 1990. xv/198 pp. $10.95 pb.

Rice worked on this commentary while team-teaching a class on preaching from 1 Kings. Thus, it is not surprising that there is a strong focus on both praxis and interpretation. This twofold concern is in keeping with the purpose of the series. Attention should be particularly directed to the frequent "theological reflection" sections in the commentary. LM****

Robinson, J. *The First Book of Kings.* CBC. Cambridge, 1972. xi/259 pp. $14.95 pb. *The Second Book of Kings.* CBC. Cambridge, 1976. xi/256 pp. $14.95 pb.

Robinson gives a concise summary of the historical background of the book. He connects its composition with the Deuteronomic reform. He writes in an easy-to-read style. Moderately critical. LM***

Chronicles

Allen, L. C. *1, 2 Chronicles.* CC. Word, 1987. 445 pp. $19.99 hb.

This is an excellent volume for laypeople, pastors, and other Christian leaders. There is deep research behind this well-written volume. LM****

✗ Braun, R. *1 Chronicles*. WBC. Word, 1986. xlv/311 pp. $22.99 hb.

A very helpful discussion of all aspects of the book. Good bibliographies, sensitive exegesis, and helpful comments on Old Testament theology. MS****

Curtis, E. L. *Chronicles*. ICC. T. and T. Clark, 1910. xxii/534 pp. $29.99 hb.

Curtis has a low view of Chronicles' historical value. He believes it is unhistorical. He does not prize Chronicles' priestly theology. He does provide a scholarly and extensive discussion of the text of Chronicles, but this is dated. S*

DeVries, S. J. *1 and 2 Chronicles*. FOTL. Eerdmans, 1989. xv/439 pp. $27.95 hb.

As with the other commentaries in the series, DeVries concentrates on the structure, genre, and intention of the book. This volume is up-to-date and provides a good perspective on contemporary scholarly opinion on the book. The bibliographies are of special value. S***

✗ Dillard, R. B. *II Chronicles*. WBC. Word, 1987. xxiii/323 pp. $24.95 hb.

This commentary makes the Book of 2 Chronicles come alive. It is superb in its analysis of the theological message of the book in the background of its composition in the post-exilic period. It is one of the few OT commentaries that explore connections with the New Testament. MS*****

McConville, J. G. *I and II Chronicles*. DSB. Westminster, 1984. 280 pp. $14.95 hb./$7.95 pb.

This commentary is an interesting and solid exposition of an often-neglected book. McConville is sensitive to theology and application. LM****

Myers, J. M. *1 and 2 Chronicles*. AB. 2 vols. Doubleday, 1965. xciv/241 pp. $14.00 hb.; xxxvi/267 pp. $16.00 hb.

Myers concentrates on issues of history and text. Of very little help in the area of theology. Recent commentaries are much better. S**

Wilcock, M. *The Message of Chronicles*. BST. Inter-Varsity, 1987. 288 pp. $9.95 pb.

Wilcock's popular commentary on Chronicles makes much of the fact that the biblical book is sermonic history. Wilcock's writing style is good and he competently brings out the ancient text's message for today. LM****

Williamson, H. G. M. *1 and 2 Chronicles*. NCB. Eerdmans, 1982. xix/428 pp. $14.95 pb.

In spite of the limitations of the series, this is a very good commentary. Williamson is a well known expert in postexilic matters and brings his formidable knowledge to bear on the text of Chronicles. MS****

Ezra

Batten, L. W. *Ezra and Nehemiah*. ICC. T. and T. Clark, 1913. xv/384 pp. $29.95 hb.

Batten represents the best of turn-of-the-century critical scholarship. He argues that Ezra–Nehemiah comes from the same school as Chronicles. Occasionally, he attempts to undo what he calls "the mischief of the Redactor" by transposing verses. S**

Blenkinsopp. J. *Ezra–Nehemiah*. OTL. Westminster, 1988. 366 pp. $29.95 hb.

Blenkinsopp is one of the leading scholars of the postexilic period, and his erudition comes to the fore in this excellent volume. He informs the reader of contemporary scholarship, but does not always agree with the current opinion (see, for instance, his view on the relation of these books to the Chronicler). He also asserts the need for diachronic analysis as well as a more literary or canonical approach. MS****

Brockington, L. H. *Ezra, Nehemiah and Esther.* NCB. Eerdmans, 1969. 189 pp. $12.95 pb.

Brockington's introduction displays a typical critical approach to the book. His comments on the text are sparse as is usual in this series. MS**

X   Clines, D. J. A. *Ezra, Nehemiah, Esther.* NCB. Eerdmans, 1984. 342 pp. $8.95 pb.

In his typical manner, Clines presents a carefully and thoroughly researched commentary. His writing is both scholarly and clear. He carefully presents the important and debated issues of historical background. There is also an excellent study of Esther's historicity. LM****

Coggins, R. J. *The Books of Ezra and Nehemiah.* CBC. Cambridge, 1976. xi/150 pp.

Coggins presents a concise, simple critical perspective. He argues for a close connection between the Chronicler and Ezra–Nehemiah. He notes some historical problems. LM***

Fensham, F. C. *The Books of Ezra and Nehemiah*. NICOT. Eerdmans, 1982. xiii/288 pp. $19.95 hb.

This commentary is traditional in its approach to these two books. For instance, it accepts the view that Ezra arrived in Palestine before Nehemiah in 458 B.C. Fensham further argues that the Chronicler was responsible for both Ezra and Nehemiah. The emphasis of this volume is on history and culture, but other aspects like philology and theology are treated as well. MS****

Holmgren, F. C. *Ezra and Nehemiah*. ITC. Eerdmans, 1987. xvii/167 pp. $10.95 pb.

This is a theological enquiry into Ezra–Nehemiah with an eye toward their significance for today. It presents a moderately critical approach. It is easy and stimulating to read. LM***

Kidner, D. *Ezra and Nehemiah*. TOTC. Inter-Varsity, 1979. 174 pp. $14.95 hb./$8.95 pb.

This volume is similar in approach to the Fensham commentary, but much less scholarly in tone (although the scholarship is there to back it up). It is thus easy to read and emphasizes theology and history. LM****

McConville, J. G. *Ezra, Nehemiah and Esther*. DSB. Westminster, 1985. xii/197 pp. $14.95 hb./$7.95 pb.

This volume is readable and scholarly without being overly academic. McConville is excellent at both revealing the books' meaning in their Old Testament context and explaining their relevance for today. LM****

Myers, J. M. *Ezra, Nehemiah*. AB. Doubleday, 1965. lxxxiii/267 pp. $16.00 hb.

Myers concentrates on a critical reconstruction of the time period reflected in these two books. The commentary is weak in the areas of philology, literary structure, style, and theology. S*

Williamson, H. G. M. *Ezra–Nehemiah*. WBC. Word, 1985. xix/428 pp. $14.95 hb.

This is a comprehensive, scholarly commentary written by a highly competent evangelical scholar. Williamson is a lecturer at Cambridge University and his research speciality is postexilic literature. Although scholarly, this book is helpful to laypeople as well. MS*****

Nehemiah

Blenkinsopp, J. *Ezra–Nehemiah*. OTL. Westminster, 1988.

See under Ezra.

Brockington, L. H. *Ezra, Nehemiah and Esther*. NCB. Eerdmans, 1969.

See under Ezra.

Holmgren, F. C. *Ezra and Nehemiah*. ITC. Eerdmans, 1987.

See under Ezra.

Kidner, D. *Ezra and Nehemiah*. TOTC. Inter-Varsity, 1979.

See under Ezra.

McConville, J. G. *Ezra, Nehemiah and Esther*. DSB. Westminster, 1985.

See under Ezra.

Myers, J. M. *Ezra, Nehemiah*. AB. Doubleday, 1965.

See under Ezra.

Williamson, H. G. M. *Ezra–Nehemiah*. WBC. Word, 1985.

See under Ezra.

Esther

Baldwin, J. G. *Esther*. TOTC. Inter-Varsity, 1984. 126 pp. $14.95 hb./$8.95 pb.

Baldwin combines a keen literary and theological sense with a firm and intelligent opinion concerning the book's historicity. The commentary is well written and based upon thorough research. LM****

Brockington, L. H. *Ezra, Nehemiah and Esther.* NCB. Eerdmans, 1969.

See under Ezra.

Coggins, R. J., and S. P. Re'emi. *Nahum, Obadiah, Esther: Israel among the Nations.* ITC. Eerdmans, 1985.

See under Obadiah.

McConville, J. G. *Ezra, Nehemiah and Esther.* DSB. Westminster, 1985.

See under Ezra.

Moore, C. A. *Esther.* AB. Doubleday, 1971. xiv/118 pp. $14.00 hb.

A competent commentary on the book from a nonevangelical perspective. There is a lengthy introductory section with helpful discussions of the problematic issues of canonicity and historicity. The commentary section proper is more balanced than some of the others (for instance, Myers on Chronicles) in the series. MS**

Murphy, R. E. *Job, Proverbs, Ruth, Canticles, Ecclesiastes, Esther.* FOTL. Eerdmans, 1981.

See under Job.

Paton, L. B. *The Book of Esther.* ICC. T. and T. Clark, 1908. xvii/339 pp. $29.95 hb.

Paton provides a large introduction, devoting much attention to text-critical matters. He is skeptical that Esther has any
historical worth. An interesting discussion from a critical perspective on Purim is the only valuable aspect of the commentary. S*

Job

Andersen, F. I. *Job*. TOTC. Inter-Varsity, 1976. 294 pp.
$14.95 hb./$8.95 pb.

This is one of the best conservative commentaries on the
book. It is limited by the length restrictions of the series, but
still extremely valuable as a lay commentary. LM***

Bergant, D. *Job, Ecclesiastes*. OTM. Michael Glazier, 1982.
295 pp. $12.95 hb./$9.95 pb.

A good popularly written and moderately critical commentary on the Book of Job. In terms of exposition, Bergant "has
decided to favor those themes, images and literary forms that
cluster around the broad concept of order" (p. 23). See also
under Ecclesiastes. LM***

Clines, D. J. A. *Job 1–20*. WBC. Word, 1989. cxi/501 pp.
$24.99 hb.

Clines has written a stimulating and insightful commentary
on the book. It is stimulating in the sense that it will get the
reader thinking about the book and its issues. It is provoca-
tively written. It is particularly strong in literary and theological analysis. The bibliographies are incredibly good. If a library
only has one commentary on Job, this one should be it (of
course, it covers only the first twenty chapters). MS*****

Dhorme, E. *A Commentary on the Book of Job*. Nelson, 1984 (orig. 1926). ccxxiv/675 pp.

The commentary, although old (originally published in 1926 in French), remains useful because of its careful study and close reading. However, much water has gone under the bridge of Old Testament studies, particularly in respect to the reading and translation of poetry. S**

Driver, S. R., and G. B. Gray. *Job*. ICC. T. and T. Clark, 1921. lxxviii/360 pp. $29.95 hb.

This volume was begun by Driver who, when he died in 1914, bequeathed its completion to Gray. The latter actually did most of the work. Gray indicates in the introduction that he and Driver believe that the original Job excluded, among smaller passages, Job 28 (the poem on wisdom) and the Elihu speech. Very technical, but occasionally helpful notes for the scholar. S***

Gibson, J. C. L. *Job*. DSB. Westminster, 1985. ix/284 pp. $16.95 hb./$8.95 pb.

Gibson honestly reports that even after several decades of study he still struggles with the meaning of the Book of Job. Although from a critical perspective, his comments will help readers struggle through this difficult biblical book themselves. LM***

Gordis, R. *The Book of Job: Commentary, New Translation and Special Studies*. Ktav, 1978. xxxiii/602 pp. $45.00 hb.

This commentary represents years of research preceded by numerous articles and a full-length book on Job. The author provides a detailed exegesis, textual study, and philological analysis. He also provides forty-two special studies on selected topics. While definitely within the critical tradition, he is moderate and looks at the book as a whole. MS****

Habel, N. C. *The Book of Job*. OTL. Westminster, 1985. 586 pp. $39.95 hb.

Habel has produced a major critical commentary on the Book of Job. It is a fairly well rounded commentary, but it concentrates particularly on literary features and theology. While Habel is aware of the questions surrounding the unity of Job, he treats it as a finished whole. MS***

Hartley, J. E. *The Book of Job*. NICOT. Eerdmans, 1988. xiv/591 pp. $27.95 hb.

This is one of the most recent commentaries on Job and it is a major contribution to the study of the book. This is because it examines all the facets of the book, not necessarily because it is terribly original. It is solidly evangelical in its approach. Very well-researched. MS***

X   Janzen, J. G. *Job*. Interp. John Knox, 1990. viii/273 pp. $19.95 hb.

In keeping with the parameters of the series, Janzen concentrates on theological significance and contemporary relevance. He does his job admirably, basing his work on an appraisal of such works as Pope and Gordis, but often presenting new ideas. He makes a small, yet significant shift away from the question "Why do the innocent suffer?" to "Why are the righteous pious?" Very helpful and stimulating. LM****

McKenna, D. L. *Job*. CC. Word, 1986. 331 pp. $19.99 hb.

McKenna concentrates on Job's "faith-development." This is a distortion of the book that shows Job moving away and not toward God in the dialogues. McKenna appropriately examines the book as it anticipates Jesus Christ. LM**

Murphy, R. E. *Wisdom Literature: Job, Proverbs, Ruth, Canticles, Ecclesiastes, Esther*. FOTL. Eerdmans, 1981. 185 pp. $16.95 pb.

This is the first volume to appear in the FOTL series. Although proportionately shorter than others, it is still full of information and certainly one of the best in the series. Perhaps it is more useable than the others because it is less technical. Murphy is also a very clear writer who is concerned about the meaning of the text. The bibliographies are great (characteristic of the series). S****

Pope, M. H. *Job*. AB. Doubleday, 1965. lxxxviii/409 pp. $20.00 hb.

As with many of the Anchor Bible commentaries, this one's strength is its philological analysis. Pope is one of the very best scholars of Northwest Semitic languages and, unlike Dahood, is a very sound practitioner of comparative Semitics. This is a good solid commentary, but not brilliant like his Song of Songs commentary. MS***

Rowley, H. H. *Job*. NCB. Eerdmans, 1970. xix/281 pp. $10.95 pb.

Rowley represents the best of British critical scholarship of the past generation. He was a prolific and knowledgeable writer. He offers thorough discussion of many critical issues and argues for a composite approach to the Book of Job. MS***

Selms, A. van. *Job.* TI. Eerdmans, 1985. vii/160 pp. $10.95 pb.

This commentary is a concise, competent reflection upon the theology of the book. However, money is better spent on larger commentaries that are more well-rounded. M**

Thomas, D. *Book of Job.* Kregel, 1982 (orig. 1878). 484 pp. $14.95 hb.

Older commentaries on Job are automatically deficient because they do not take into account recent developments in textual criticism, philology, and Near Eastern studies. However, there are some homiletical helps. LM**

Psalms

Alden, R. *Psalms.* EBC. 3 vols. Moody, 1974–76. 124, 124, 112 pp. $5.95 (ea.) pb.

In keeping with the series, this volume is popularly written, short, and conservative. It is informed by scholarly research. L***

Allen, L. C. *Psalms 101–150.* WBC. Word, 1983. xx/342 pp. $22.95 hb.

This commentary covers the last third of the Psalter. It is particularly helpful in two areas: language and structure. Allen has very good insight into how the structure of a psalm contributes to its message. While he is good at getting at the message of the psalm in its Old Testament setting, he is very slow in seeing the connection between the text and the New Testament. MS****

Anderson, A. A. *Psalms.* NCB. 2 vols. Eerdmans, 1972. 966 pp. $10.95 (ea.) pb.

This is a good modern treatment of the psalms. It is a little too brief and tied to the restrictive NCB format. The Allen and Craigie volumes are much better. M***

Briggs, C. A. *Psalms.* ICC. 2 vols. T. and T. Clark, 1906. cx/422 pp. $29.95; vii/572 pp. $29.95 hb.

This is a highly technical, fairly dated discussion of the psalms. It is more interesting from the perspective of the history of interpretation than for exposition. S**

Craigie, P. *Psalms 1–50.* WBC. Word, 1983. 375 pp. $22.95 hb.

This is the first of the three psalms commentaries in the Word series. As the first in the series, this volume contains introductory material concerning authorship, use, style, and theology. Craigie's commentary is the best of the modern commentaries on the psalms in matters of language and Old Testament background and message. He is a well known Ugaritic specialist and is able to cut through the benefits and pitfalls of recent research into the connections between Ugaritic and biblical literature. Two weaknesses of the commentary are his poetical comments and the connections that he draws (or fails to draw) with the New Testament message. This commentary is a must-buy for a serious student of the psalms, but it should be complemented by a commentary that is strong in its theological insight (like Kidner). MS*****

Dahood, M. J. *Psalms*. AB. Doubleday, 1965, 1968, 1970. xlvi/329 pp. $18.00; xxx/399 pp. $18.00; liv/490 pp. $22.00 hb.

Dahood is (in)famous for his use of Northwest Semitic (particularly Ugaritic) in his study of the psalms. While there is no doubt that cognate languages have helped our understanding of the psalms, Dahood has overused them in his commentary. There is no methodological control, and even Ugaritic scholars cannot evaluate his arguments. Nonspecialists will be at a total loss. In short, this commentary is very eccentric. S*

Dickson, D. *Psalms*. Banner of Truth, 1959 (orig. 1653–55). 538 pp. $22.95 hb.

This commentary is written in archaic English. Most people will benefit more from the recent commentaries. LM**

Eaton, J. H. *Psalms*. TBC. SCM, 1967. 317 pp.

A popular, brief commentary by one of today's leading experts on the psalms. He assigns a large role to the king. LM****

Gerstenberger, E. S. *Psalms*. 2 vols. (only vol. 1 is out). FOTL. Eerdmans, 1989. xv/260 pp. $24.95.

Excellent tool for scholars because of its scholarship and bibliographies. It is extremely doubtful that ministers or laypeople will have much use for this series. S****

Kidner, D. *Psalms 1–72* and *Psalms 73–150*. TOTC. Inter-Varsity, 1973, 1975. x/492 pp. $14.95 (ea.) hb./$8.95 (ea.). pb.

Kidner has written two volumes on the psalms. Unfortunately, they are very brief. This is compensated for by Kidner's ability to write concisely. Thus, in spite of its brevity, this commentary is highly recommended for its theological insight and practical bent. The discussion of the Hebrew text is minimal and is not intended to be very sophisticated. However, the introductory material, particularly the discussion of the meaning of the difficult words in the titles, is very helpful. This commentary is well worth its price. LM****

Knight, G. A. F. *Psalms*. DSB. 2 vols. Westminster, 1982. 350 pp. $12.95 hb./$7.95 pb.; 384 pp. $15.95 hb./$8.95 pb.

This volume, like the others in DSB, is theologically sensitive from a Christian perspective. It is moderate in its criticism, devoting more attention to the elucidation of meaning than to other aspects of study like poetics or the Near Eastern background. LM****

Plumer, W. W. *Psalms*. Banner of Truth, 1975 (orig. 1867). 1211 pp. $33.95.

So much has been learned since Plumer's time that the only use of the volume is for an occasional theological insight. LM**

Rogerson, J. W., and J. W. McKay. *Psalms*. CBC. Cambridge, 1977. xi/243 pp. $37.50 hb./$12.95 pb.; xi/193 pp. $37.50 hb./$11.95 pb.

The authors have tried to "strike a balance between the spiritual, historical, form-critical and cultic approaches." They depart from the NEB in that they believe that the titles, although added later, have something to add to our understanding of the psalms. LM***

Weiser, A. *The Psalms*. OTL. Westminster, 1962. 841 pp. $29.95 hb.

While not strongly recommended for purchase, this commentary is often theologically insightful. One must be aware of the neo-orthodox perspective from which the author is writing and also his belief that all of the psalms fit into an annual covenant renewal ceremony. Weiser is correct to see a close connection between the psalms and the covenant, but mistaken to reconstruct an annual festival with which to connect them. This theory is a definite improvement over Mowinckel's enthronement festival, however. Weiser is a theological commentator on the psalms. There is little help in the areas of language or structure. LM**

Williams, D. M. *Psalms*. CC. 2 vols. Word, 1986, 1989. 493, 543 pp. $19.99 (ea.) hb.

Williams does his scholarly homework well as he attempts to help ministers and other Christian leaders communicate the message of the psalms in their Old Testament setting. He includes some anecdotes and interesting illustrations. LM****

Proverbs

Aitken, K. T. *Proverbs*. DSB. Westminster, 1986. 276 pp. $15.95 hb./$8.95 pb.

The introduction to this volume is one of the more critical of the series, although the bulk of the commentary provides helpful information. Interestingly, Aitken orders the material in Proverbs 10 and following in a topical rather than textual format. LM***

Alden, R. *Proverbs*. Baker, 1983. 222 pp. $8.95 pb.

This is a devotional commentary on the book. While it does discuss various translation possibilities, it is more concerned to draw applications for today. Sometimes these applications are helpful and right; others are forced and even trite. L***

Bridges, C. *Proverbs*. Banner of Truth, 1968 (orig. 1846). xv/640 pp. $18.95 hb.

Wise, practical, and scholarly are descriptive terms appropriate to this commentary written nearly a century and a half ago. From a philological point of view the commentary is dated, but it is still valuable. LM****

Hubbard, D. A. *Proverbs*. CC. Word, 1989. 487 pp.

While somewhat more scholarly in tone than other commentaries in the series, Hubbard's contribution is still quite readable and achieves the purposes of CC. The introduction highlights six principles of interpretation before beginning the commentary proper. Hubbard gives important guidelines to the proper understanding of the forms of speech and literary devices of the book. The section on Proverbs 10ff. orders the discussion by topic rather than verse-by-verse. LM****

Kidner, D. *Proverbs*. TOTC. Inter-Varsity, 1964. 192 pp. $14.95 hb./$8.95 pb.

This small commentary is packed with helpful insight and comments on the text. It is exegetically sensitive, theologically helpful, and orthodox. However, for serious study of Proverbs it should be supplemented by a fuller commentary like McKane's. LM****

McKane, W. *Proverbs: A New Approach*. OTL. Westminster, 1970. xvii/670 pp.

This commentary is a significant contribution to the study of Proverbs, even if the critical conclusions are difficult to appreciate. McKane differentiates the instruction genre of 1–9, 22:17–24:22, 31:1–9 from the sentence literature of 10–22:16, 24:23–34, and 25–29. However, this commentary is invaluable for the study of the language of Proverbs. The way to use it is to turn to McKane's translation on pages 211–61, where he references his discussion of individual verses. A further debatable conclusion of his study is his division of the sentence literature into three classes. A must for scholarly enquiry into Proverbs, but of doubtful value to the layperson or pastor. MS****

Murphy, R. E. *Job, Proverbs, Ruth, Canticles, Ecclesiastes, Esther.* FOTL. Eerdmans, 1981.

See under Job.

Scott, R. B. Y. *Proverbs, Ecclesiastes*. AB. Doubleday, 1965. liii/257 pp. $18.00 hb.

This is not one of the better commentaries in the Anchor Bible series. It represents a classical critical approach to Proverbs. It is not particularly strong in any area of research. S*

Toy, C. H. *Proverbs*. ICC. T. and T. Clark, 1899. xxxvi/554 pp. $29.95 hb.

Toy was one of the leading scholars of the turn of the century, but his commentary is now dated in its critical methodology and conclusions. S**

Whybray, R. N. *The Book of Proverbs*. CBC. Cambridge, 1972. x/197 pp. $10.95 pb.

A good, competent study of the book from a critical perspective. Whybray distinguishes secular from religious proverbs. He studies the book in its ancient Near Eastern setting. LM**

Ecclesiastes

Barton, G. A. *Ecclesiastes*. ICC. T. and T. Clark, 1908. xiv/212 pp. $29.95.

Barton is a good example of a turn-of-the-century critical scholar. This commentary is very detailed, and certainly not for the nonscholar. Barton has thorough text-critical discussions and tries to argue a close connection between Ecclesiastes and Greek thought. S*

Bergant, D. *Job, Ecclesiastes*. OTM. Michael Glazier, 1982.

See under Job.

Bridges, C. *Ecclesiastes*. Banner of Truth, 1961 (orig. 1860). xvi/319 pp. $16.95 hb.

Bridges takes a traditional approach to the book, arguing that the repentant aged Solomon is the author. Bridges begins with the premise that the Scriptures cannot contain anything that is not from God. Properly applied, this is a true principle;

however, the Scriptures do quote dubious theology (Job's friends) and Bridges does not take into account the possibility that much of the book represents the Preacher's skeptical teaching—teaching that is redirected and challenged at the end. Nonetheless, with Bridges' practical and christological bent there is much in this commentary that is profitable today. LM****

Crenshaw, J. L. *Ecclesiastes*. OTL. Westminster, 1987. 192 pp. $19.95 hb.

Crenshaw's approach may be described as moderately critical. However, this is an excellent commentary. It is not too technical (one gets the feeling that Crenshaw is holding himself back), but it is a profound approach to the book. Highly recommended. MS****

Davidson, R. *Ecclesiastes and Song of Solomon*. DSB. Westminster, 1986. 168 pp. $14.95 hb./$7.95 pb.

This volume is one of the more critical of the series, especially on such issues as the date and composition of Ecclesiastes. Nonetheless, it provides a helpful and nondogmatic perspective. LM****

Eaton, Michael A. *Ecclesiastes*. TOTC. Inter-Varsity, 1983. 159 pp. $14.95 hb./$8.95 pb.

Eaton writes well, with a nontechnical audience in mind. He has many good insights into the text, but the commentary is marred by his view that the orthodoxy of Ecclesiastes can be preserved only by turning Qohelet into a "preacher of joy"— quite an exegetical trick. LM**

Fox, M. V. *Qohelet and His Contradictions.* Almond, 1989. 384 pp. $19.95 pb.

This book may be divided into two parts. The first half treats the book as a whole and offers some tantalizing essays on some key themes, arguing for instance that the key phrase of the book is not "vanity" or "meaninglessness" but rather "absurdity." The second part of the book is a commentary with an emphasis on philology, textual criticism, the book's structure, and interpretation. Fox's idea of Ecclesiastes as a framed monologue is very provocative. MS****

Ginsburg, C. D. *The Song of Songs and Coheleth.* Ktav, 1970 (orig. 1857). xliv/528 pp. $79.95 hb.

Ginsburg was an extremely learned scholar who was well versed in both Christian and Jewish scholarship. His approach is dated, but the prolegomenon, written by S. Blank, attempts to bring certain discussions up to date. S***

Goldberg, L. *Ecclesiastes.* Zondervan, 1983. 144 pp. $6.95 pb.

This volume is a popularly written, conservative approach to the book. But its particular approach, much like Kaiser's, is misguided. L**

Gordis, R. *Koheleth: The Man and His World.* Schocken, 1951. x/421 pp. $10.95 pb.

This is becoming one of the classics on the book. It is a treasury of previous research. Gordis is not only thorough in his research but also meticulous in his thinking. He provides a new translation. S****

Hubbard, D. A. *Beyond Futility.* Eerdmans, 1976.

This short, lay-oriented commentary is extremely insightful, particularly in its comments on how Christ moves beyond the futility of Qohelet. LM****

Kaiser, W. C., Jr., *Ecclesiastes: Total Life.* EBC. Moody, 1979. 128 pp. $6.95 pb.

Kaiser has written a very readable commentary on the Book of Ecclesiastes. Unfortunately, he takes an untenable approach to the book, turning the main speaker Qohelet into an orthodox "preacher of joy." LM**

Kidner, D. *A Time to Mourn and a Time to Dance.* InterVarsity, 1976. 110 pp. $9.95 pb.

This commentary is very popular, but may be the best on the Book of Ecclesiastes. It is well written and sensible in its approach to Ecclesiastes. Shows application to life as well. LM****

Loader, J. A. *Ecclesiastes: A Practical Commentary.* TI. Trans. J. Vriend. Eerdmans, 1986. vi/136 pp. $9.95 pb.

As commentaries on Ecclesiastes go, Loader's is one of the better ones. However, the last word is far from being said. Loader is a sophisticated biblical scholar who is well known for his structuralist analysis of Ecclesiastes. In this work he keeps away from obscure academic discussions. While he gives some helpful advice on how to view the book's connection with the New Testament, he really does not have a good grasp on the genre of the book as a whole. MS***

Murphy, R. E. *Job, Proverbs, Ruth, Canticles, Ecclesiastes, Esther.* FOTL. Eerdmans, 1981.

See under Job.

Scott, R. B. Y. *Proverbs, Ecclesiastes.* AB. Doubleday, 1965. xii/257 pp. $18.00 hb.

See under Proverbs. Ecclesiastes is treated very briefly, almost like an afterthought. S*

Whybray, R. N. *Ecclesiastes.* NCB. Eerdmans, 1989. xxiii/179 pp. $13.95 pb.

Whybray, a prolific and respected English Old Testament scholar, has written on Ecclesiastes before, most notably in his article "Qohelet: Preacher of Joy" (*JSOT* 23 [1982]: 87–98). Here, as there, he leans toward an interpretation that sees Qohelet as a realist who, in spite of clearly seeing all the problems of a world living under the effects of the curse, nonetheless believes that God wants his people to enjoy life. Whybray argues that Ecclesiastes is late (3d cent. B.C.) and under some Greek influence. MS****

Song of Songs

Burrowes, G. *Song of Solomon.* Banner of Truth, 1958 (orig. 1853). 527 pp. $12.95 hb.

This antiquated commentary presents an allegorical approach to the text. It is best avoided except for its historical interest. S*

Carr, G. L. *Song of Songs.* TOTC. Inter-Varsity, 1984. 175 pp. $14.95 hb./$8.95 pb.

This is a good popular exposition of the Song. Much scholarly research stands behind it. Carr takes a flexible approach to authorship and makes an adequate presentation of alternative approaches to the book. He himself advocates a "natural reading." LM***

Davidson, R. *Ecclesiastes and Song of Solomon*. DSB. Westminster, 1986. viii/162 pp. $14.95 hb./$7.95 pb.

See under Ecclesiastes. Davidson rightly takes the view that the Song is a collection of love poems. He gives a helpful analysis of the imagery of the book. LM****

Dillow, S. J. *Solomon on Sex*. Nelson, 1977. 197 pp. $5.95 pb.

This commentary is very popular and should not be consulted in serious study of the book. It takes the view that Solomon is the author and the chief subject. It reads like a Christian sex manual, and should not be confused with a commentary. L*

Ginsburg, C. D. *The Song of Songs and Coheleth*. Ktav, 1970 (orig. 1857). xliv/528 pp. $79.95 hb.

See under Ecclesiastes.

Glickman, S. C. *A Song for Lovers*. Inter-Varsity, 1976. 188 pp. $7.95 pb.

This volume is similar in intention to the Dillow volume, but is based on more substantial research and a more mature understanding of the book. LM**

Knight, G. A. F., and F. W. Golka. *The Song of Songs and Jonah*. ITC. Eerdmans, 1988. ix/136 pp. $10.95 hb.

Knight's contribution is an interesting reassertion of the divine-human aspects of the relationship depicted in that book. LM***

Murphy, R. E. *Job, Proverbs, Ruth, Canticles, Ecclesiastes, Esther*. FOTL. Eerdmans, 1981.

See under Job.

Murphy, R. E. *The Song of Songs*. Hermeneia. Fortress, 1990. xxii/227 pp. $21.95 hb.

Murphy provides an excellent critical reading of the text. He emphasizes its final form and is concerned with theological issues. His lengthy introduction gives a helpful survey of the history of interpretation, issues of prosody, and basic interpretative approach. MS****

Pope, M. H. *Song of Songs*. AB. Doubleday, 1977. xxi/743 pp. $22.00 hb.

This is one of the best commentaries written on any book of the Bible. It contains a wealth of linguistic, literary, and historical information. The history of interpretation, comparative sections, and fifty-five-page bibliography are worth the price of the book. Pope fairly represents positions different from his own. His overall approach to the book as connected with the love and death cults of the ancient world leaves much to be desired, but is interesting. MS*****

Isaiah

Clements, R. E. *Isaiah 1–39*. NCB. Eerdmans, 1980. xvi/301 pp. $8.95 pb.

Clements is an evangelical who practices a moderate higher criticism. He is one of the most prolific British writers in the field of Old Testament. He has a good writing style and practices sensitive exegesis. However, his critical perspective mars many of his insights. MS***

Gray, G. B. *Isaiah 1–27*. ICC. T. and T. Clark, 1912. ci/472 pp. $29.95 hb.

This is a detailed and scholarly presentation of turn-of-the century critical thought on the Book of Isaiah. S**

Herbert, A. S. *The Book of the Prophet Isaiah*. CBC. 2 vols. Cambridge, 1975. x/219, ix/204 pp. $27.95 hb./$13.95 pb.

Herbert gives considerable attention to the historical background and the phenomenology of prophecy. LM**

Kaiser, O. *Isaiah 1–39*. OTL. 2 vols. Westminster, 1972. xx/170, xix/412 pp. $19.95 (ea.) hb.

Kaiser represents the best of German critical scholarship on the Book of Isaiah. S***

Knight, G. A. F. *Isaiah 40–55: Servant Theology*. ITC. Eerdmans, 1984. ix/204 pp. *Isaiah 55–66: The New Israel*. ITC. Eerdmans, 1985. xvii/126 pp. $10.95 (ea.) pb.

Although he argues against an eighth-century date for the prophecy, Knight brackets historical-critical concerns. He shows great sensitivity to exegetical and theological issues. LM***

McKenzie, J. L. *Second Isaiah*. AB. Doubleday, 1968. lxxi/225 pp. $14.00 hb.

Although its title might lead the reader to think otherwise, McKenzie actually comments on both what he calls second Isaiah and third Isaiah. The latter he thinks is made up of miscellaneous oracles from anonymous sources. There are better commentaries on the subject, in both the critical and evangelical camps. S**

North, C. R. *Isaiah 40–55*. TBC. SCM, 1952. 158 pp.

North was one of the greatest critical interpreters of Isaiah of the past generation with a particular interest in the servant songs. He brings incredible expertise to this popular commentary. His approach to the servant songs is particularly interesting and noteworthy. M****

Oswalt, J. *Isaiah 1–39*. NICOT. Eerdmans, 1986. xiii/746 pp. $29.95 hb.

This volume is solidly conservative and well researched. Oswalt is producing a second volume on the rest of the book. MS****

Ridderbos, J. *Isaiah*. BSC. Zondervan, 1985. 580 pp. $20.95 hb.

This commentary is a translation of a Dutch original first published in 1950/51. It is oriented toward the minister. Ridderbos is a top-flight scholar. He accepts the essential unity of Isaiah, although admitting some secondary glosses added by Isaiah's disciples. The commentary has the advantages and disadvantages of a one-volume commentary on such a long and complex book. It is easy to digest, but often superficial (largely due to length constraints). It is written from a Reformed, conservative perspective. MS***

Sawyer, J. F. A. *Isaiah*. DSB. 2 vols. Westminster, 1984, 1986. 280 pp. $14.95 hb./$7.95 pb.

Sawyer accepts the common critical understanding of Isaiah as composed by different individuals inspired by the original eighth-century prophet. However, in the commentary proper he does not deal with such historical issues; rather, he concentrates on the meaning of the text for today. LM***

Watts, J. D. W. *Isaiah*. WBC. Word, 1985, 1987. lvii/449 pp. $24.95 hb.; xxiii/385 pp. $24.95 hb.

Watts has written a commentary on the canonical form of the book. He is not concerned with prehistory, but interprets the book in its present form. This form points to a fifth-century date for the book, although the author used materials from earlier (eighth-century) settings. Watts proposes a twelvefold structure to the book (in two [1–39; 40–66] parts) that follows a kind of chronological flow. (Reviewers question his approach here.) This is an interesting and provocative commentary. MS***

Westermann, C. *Isaiah 40–66*. OTL. Westminster, 1969. iv/429 pp. $21.95 hb.

This volume completes Kaiser's first two volumes in the OTL series. Westermann here offers a commentary on what he calls deutero- and trito-Isaiah. Westermann is always insightful and this commentary should not be ignored because of its critical basis. MS****

Whybray, R. N. *Isaiah 40–66*. NCB. Eerdmans, 1980. 301 pp. $10.95 pb.

Whybray divides his commentary between chapters 40–55 (Deutero-Isaiah) and 56–66 (Trito-Isaiah). He carefully describes the historical background of Deutero-Isaiah in the Neo-Babylonian period. He applies the form-critical method to the elucidation of the text. His exposition is clear and scholarly, which is what we expect from Whybray. The format of the series, however, is very restricting. LM***

Widyapranawa, S. H. *Isaiah 1–39: The Lord Is Savior.* ITC. Eerdmans, 1990. xiv/266 pp. $14.95 pb.

This commentary is produced by an Old Testament professor from Indonesia with the hope that he might set the teaching of the prophet within a third world perspective. While he does a competent job of interpretation, there is not much practical application to contemporary society. The introduction is virtually nonexistent. LM***

Young, E. J. *The Book of Isaiah*. 3 vols. Eerdmans, 1965, 1969, 1972. xii/534, 604, 579 pp.

Young's commentary was originally in the NICOT series, but the series floundered after his work came out and has only been revived in the past decade (without Young's commentary; see Oswalt). Young was a meticulous and detailed scholar, which is evident in his work here. He is a better philologist than literary scholar or biblical theologian, but the commentary is well worth the money. The commentary takes a very conservative approach to Isaiah. Young's writing style is tedious. MS**

Jeremiah

Boadt, L. *Jeremiah 1–25*. OTM. Michael Glazier, 1982. $15.95 hb./$10.95 pb. *Jeremiah 26–52, Habakkuk, Zephaniah, Nahum*. OTM. Michael Glazier, 1982. $15.95 hb. /$10.95 pb.

A popular theological commentary on four prophets from the latter half of the seventh century. Boadt treats them together because they offer different perspectives on the same historical events. LM***

Bright, J. *Jeremiah*. AB. Doubleday, 1965. cxliv/372 pp. $20.00 hb.

This is one of the better commentaries on Jeremiah, although it is written from a moderately critical angle. Bright has good theological and literary sense. One disconcerting feature of this commentary is its arrangement. Bright has chosen to depart from Jeremiah's more topical arrangement and has commented on the text in a reconstructed chronological order. MS***

Carroll, R. P. *The Book of Jeremiah*. OTL. Westminster, 1986. 874 pp. $38.95 hb.

Carroll includes an excellent bibliography. His commentary emphasizes a redaction-critical approach to the book in an attempt to reconcile what he calls the "disparate *personae* of Jeremiah represented by the various levels of tradition in it" (p. 37). S***

Clements, R. E. *Jeremiah*. Interp. John Knox, 1988. 228 pp. $17.95 hb.

Clements adopts a moderately critical approach to questions of composition and authorship. He concentrates on integrating historical background and theological message. The book is clearly written and profitable. LM***

Cunliffe-Jones, H. *Jeremiah*. TBC. Macmillan, 1961. $8.95.

The author builds on a moderately critical approach to the text in order to emphasize Jeremiah's theology and the relevance of the book for today. He also focuses on Jeremiah's personality as it is disclosed in the text. LM***

Davidson, R. *Jeremiah and Lamentations*. DSB. 2 vols. Westminster, 1983, 1985. 176 pp. $12.95 hb./$6.95 pb.; 224 pp. $14.95 hb./$7.95 pb.

Davidson devotes all of the first volume and most of the second to a study of the prophecy of Jeremiah. While he accepts a moderately critical approach to the text, he does not present critical discussions in the commentary. The result is a popularly written and helpful exposition. LM****

Guest, J. *Jeremiah, Lamentations*. CC. Word, 1988. 390 pp. $19.99 hb.

Guest writes with a good understanding of the book in its Old Testament background and awareness of its New Testament connections. His writing style is engaging and he provides insightful comment. LM***

Holladay, W. L. *Jeremiah.* 2 vols. Hermeneia. Fortress, 1986, 1989. xxii/682 pp. $44.95 hb.; xxxi/543 pp. $44.95 hb.

This is a major contribution to Jeremiah studies written from a form-critical perspective that should be consulted by everyone who does serious work on the book. Like the others in the series, it is a well presented commentary. MS****

Harrison, R. K. *Jeremiah and Lamentations.* TOTC. Inter-Varsity, 1973. 240 pp. $14.95 hb./$8.95 pb.

Due to its size restrictions, this commentary is unable to compare with some of the others as a major research tool. However, it is an excellent commentary for laypeople. The emphasis is on history, philology, and theology. LM***

McKane, W. *A Critical and Exegetical Commentary on Jeremiah 1.* ICC. T. and T. Clark, 1986. cxxii/658 pp. $49.95 hb.

This is an example of the "new generation" ICC commentaries. Not many Old Testament commentaries are out yet. They have the same critical concerns as the older series: textual criticism, philology, and historical matters. There is little theological reflection. However, since the newer volumes take into account recent changes in these volumes are more valuable than the older ones. McKane's volume has extensive text-critical and redaction-critical discussions. A must for all scholars, but just as well ignored by most laypersons and ministers. S***

Nicholson, E. W. *Jeremiah.* CBC. 2 vols. Cambridge, 1973–75. xii/220, xi/247 pp. $11.95, $12.95 pb.

The introduction helpfully reconstructs the historical background to the prophecy. Nicholson examines the literary growth of the book from Jeremiah the prophet through the Deuteronomic school. LM**

Thompson, J. A. *The Book of Jeremiah.* NICOT. Eerdmans, 1979. xii/819 pp. $29.95 hb.

Thompson takes a more traditional and evangelical approach to the book. However, he does allow for some non-Jeremiah parts. He treats Jeremiah as a real person in a definite historical setting. Well worth getting. MS****

Lamentations

Davidson, R. *Jeremiah* (vol. 2) *and Lamentations.* DSB. Westminster, 1985.

Davidson's comments on Lamentations are vivid and concise. He uses a number of modern analogies to bring the horror of the destruction of Jerusalem to life. See also under Jeremiah. LM****

Harrison, R. K. *Jeremiah and Lamentations.* TOTC. Inter-Varsity, 1973.

See under Jeremiah.

Hillers, D. R. *Lamentations.* AB. Doubleday, 1972. xlviii/116 pp. $18.00 hb.

A good commentary—in fact, probably the best on the Book of Lamentations. It does a good job elucidating the book's Near Eastern literary background. MS***

Martin-Achard, R., and S. Paul Re'emi. *Amos and Lamentations*. ITC. Eerdmans, 1984. viii/134 pp. $10.95 pb.

Re'emi gives a balanced, common-sense interpretation of Lamentations. See also under Amos. LM***

Ezekiel

Allen, L.C. *Ezekiel 20–48*. WBC. Word, 1990. xxviii/301 pp.

Brownlee's death interrupted the completion of his commentary on Ezekiel. Allen now has completed his work. Brownlee's approach was somewhat eccentric, and Allen departs from it and goes his own way. While this divergence is unfortunate, it may be the best for the series. Allen is concerned with both the final form of the book as well as its composition. In this regard, he sees himself mediating the positions represented by Greenberg and Zimmerli. MS****

Blenkinsopp, J. *Ezekiel*. Interp. John Knox, 1990. vi/242 pp. $19.95 hb.

This series, written from a moderately critical perspective, is a delight to read. It is rich in theological insight and very accessible. Blenkinsopp's commentary is no exception. In the introduction, he gives a clear explanation of his view of the process of growth of a prophetic book and applies it to Ezekiel. He focuses on religious and theological issues, with a special concentration on the presence/absence of God. LM****

Brownlee, W. H. *Ezekiel 1–19*. WBC. Word, 1986. 321 pp. $22.99 hb.

Brownlee died when his commentary reached this point. L. C. Allen finished it. Although Brownlee had a high view of Scripture, this did not prevent him from seeing considerable editorial activity and redaction over a long period of time, resulting in the book that we have before us. Yet "despite all this editorial activity, the major contents of the book of Ezekiel are genuine, and whatever editing they later received serves to emphasize the prophet's greatness" (p. xl). MS***

Carley, K. W. *The Book of the Prophet Ezekiel*. CBC. Cambridge, 1974. 331 pp.

Carley writes clearly and has produced a competent, critical commentary for the layperson. LM***

Cooke, G. A. *Ezekiel*. ICC. T. and T. Clark, 1936. xlvii/541 pp. $29.95 hb.

This volume is less tedious than most in the series. Cooke is both scholarly and thorough. His approach is critical, but tinged with piety. The survey of the historical background is comprehensive but dated. S***

Craigie, P. C. *Ezekiel*. DSB. Westminster, 1983. x/321 pp. $14.95 hb./$7.95 pb.

Craigie's brief yet helpful commentary is extremely readable. It opens up this difficult book for the interested layreader. It takes an evangelical approach to the book. LM****

Eichrodt, W. *Ezekiel*. OTL. Westminster, 1970. xiv/594 pp. $22.95 hb.

Eichrodt's study is a translation of a work originally published in German in 1965/66. Eichrodt's moderately critical approach in the main agrees with the biblical presentation of Ezekiel and his ministry. Eichrodt applies a critical methodology that he believes does reveal some non-Ezekiel passages, but what is left, in his opinion, is without a doubt original. S***

Feinberg, C. L. *The Prophecy of Ezekiel*. Moody, 1969. 286 pp. $12.95 hb.

This commentary was first produced as a series of articles in a popular evangelical magazine. Thus, the author has in mind a lay audience whose interests are primarily the theological message of the book. Feinberg's perspective is dispensationalist. L**

Greenberg, M. *Ezekiel 1–20*. AB. Doubleday, 1983. 388 pp. $18.00 hb.

This is a very interesting commentary on the Book of Ezekiel. Greenberg is well aware of what he is trying to accomplish as a commentator (see pp. 18–27). He advocates what he calls a holistic approach, which basically treats the MT as it stands and as a whole. Very stimulating. MS****

Stuart, D. *Ezekiel*. CC. Word, 1989. 426 pp. $19.99 hb.

Stuart is one of the few professional academics asked to contribute to this series. His volume has a slightly different flavor than the others. It has more actual interpretation and explanation of the text and fewer personal anecdotes. Stuart's writing style is nevertheless still quite engaging. LM****

Taylor, J. B. *Ezekiel*. TOTC. Inter-Varsity, 1969. 285 pp. $14.95 hb./$8.95 pb.

This commentary is especially designed for those who know little about Ezekiel. It is conservative and easy to read. LM**

Wevers, J. W. *Ezekiel.* NCB. Eerdmans, 1969. x/355 pp. $10.95 pb.

Wevers presents a more traditional critical approach than Greenberg and is a lot less stimulating than other critical scholars, especially Zimmerli. S**

Zimmerli, W. *Ezekiel 1 and 2.* Hermeneia. Fortress, 1979, 1982. xlvi/509, xxxiv/606 pp. $39.95 (ea.) hb.

The German original was published in 1969. An English translation was long anticipated because of Zimmerli's breadth of knowledge and incredible insight. Zimmerli represents the best of critical thought on the Book of Ezekiel. MS*****

Daniel

Anderson, R. A. *Daniel: Signs and Wonders.* ITC. Eerdmans, 1984. xvii/158 pp. $10.95 pb.

This is a competent, well written popularization of certain critical theories about Daniel. LM***

Baldwin, J. G. *Daniel.* TOTC. Inter-Varsity, 1978. 210 pp. $14.95 hb./$8.95 pb.

Although short, this commentary contains a wealth of information and careful exegetical insight. Baldwin is a balanced and sane exegete, which is important to note in a commentary on a book that attracts some wild ideas. Baldwin is solidly conservative, but not rigid. LM****

Collins, J. J. *Daniel with an Introduction to Apocalyptic Literature*. FOTL. Eerdmans, 1984. xv/120 pp. $18.95 pb.

In keeping with the purpose of the series, Collins, a recognized authority on Daniel and Old Testament apocalyptic, concentrates on the form and structure of the book. He has synthesized a tremendous amount of secondary literature in short compass as well as presenting his own interesting perspective. He assumes a critical approach to the book. S****

Ferguson, S. B. *Daniel*. CC. Word, 1988. 252 pp. $19.99 hb.

Ferguson provides a good balance of exposition and application. His narrative is spiced with helpful illustrations and anecdotes. He avoids speculation on some of the prophecies, preferring to concentrate on the theme of the "good news of the kingdom of God." Good christological focus. LM****

Goldingay, J. *Daniel*. Word, 1989. liii/351 pp. $24.95 hb.

Goldingay's is perhaps the most comprehensive commentary on Daniel listed here. He gives insight into historical, literary, and theological issues concerning the book. He also demonstrates an amazing grasp of the secondary literature. Many of his readers will be put off by some of his radical (at least for an evangelical) conclusions, most notable of which are that the stories in chapters 1–6 are fictitious and the visions are quasi-prophecies. However, it would be a major mistake to ignore this important commentary while studying Daniel. MS*****

Hartman, L. F., and A. A. Dilella. *The Book of Daniel.* AB. Doubleday, 1978. xiv/345 pp. $18.00 hb.

This is one of the skimpier volumes in the Anchor Bible series. It takes a typically critical approach to the date of the book. The exegetical comments are not that helpful. S*

Heaton, E. *Daniel.* TBC. SCM, 1956. 251 pp.

In his lengthy introduction, Heaton draws a close connection between the author of Daniel and Ben Sira, as well as the Hasideans. He argues that Daniel should be identified with the Danel of Ugaritic literature. He presents a typical argument for the late date of the book. Nonetheless, it may still be profitably read. LM****

Lacocque, A. *The Book of Daniel.* John Knox, 1979. xxvi/302 pp. $24.95 hb.

This is an English translation of a French commentary originally published in 1976. Although he does provide some helpful textual and philological notes, Lacocque is strong on theology and contemporary application (at least relatively so for a critical scholar). He adopts a traditional critical dating and interpretation. MS***

Montgomery, J. A. *Daniel.* ICC. T. and T. Clark, 1927. xxxi/488 pp. $29.95 hb.

This commentary concentrates on the building blocks of exegesis like philology and text. It becomes the basis for the theological comments of more recent commentaries as diverse as Young and Porteous. S****

Porteous, N. W. *Daniel.* OTL. Westminster, 1965. 173 pp.

Porteous concentrates on theology, not language. The commentary is shjort. Porteous adopts a critical stance toward the book. S**

Russell, D. S. *Daniel.* DSB. Westminster, 1981. 244 pp. $6.95 pb.

Russell is one of the leading critical interpreters of apocalyptic literature of the previous generation. In his introduction, he dates the book late and gives a very unsatisfactory explanation of pseudonymity. However, his insistence on the present relevance of the book (over against a speculative futuristic approach) has much to commend itself. LM***

Towner, W. S. *Daniel.* Interp. John Knox, 1984. 228 pp. $16.95 hb.

This commentary concentrates on the theology of the book and is written from a critical perspective. The writing is clear and often insightful. MS***

Wallace, R. S. *The Lord Is King: The Message of Daniel.* BST. Inter-Varsity, 1979. 200 pp. $9.95 pb.

Wallace has written a good popular exposition from an evangelical perspective. Solid research backs up his comments. The introduction provides a helpful conservative defense against a late dating of the book. LM****

Wood, L. *A Commentary on Daniel.* Zondervan, 1990 (orig. 1973). 336 pp. $14.95 pb.

Zondervan has just republished Wood's earlier work on Daniel in which he provides a scholarly defense of a premillennial approach to the book. The commentary takes a word-by-word and verse-by-verse approach. Young's commentary is to be preferred for its theological perspective and depth of scholarship, but Wood had recourse to D. J. Wiseman's *Chronicles of the Chaldean Kings,* which helped considerably in historical background. LM**

Young, E. J. *The Prophecy of Daniel.* Banner of Truth, 1949. 330 pp. $21.95 hb.

The importance of this commentary is found in its firm and intelligent conservative stance. Young polemicizes against critical and dispensationalist approaches. He is not particularly sensitive to the literary nature or biblical theology of the book, but he is an excellent language scholar. MS***

Hosea

Andersen, F. I., and D. N. Freedman. *Hosea.* AB. Doubleday, 1980. xiii/699 pp. $20.00 hb.

This massive commentary is one of the best on any biblical book. For one thing, the authors are permitted the space to do a fuller job of commenting on the Hebrew text. Both authors are well known, respected linguists. Andersen has some theological sense. The book is marred a little by a syllable-counting approach to meter. MS****

Beeby, H. D. *Hosea: Grace Abounding.* ITC. Eerdmans, 1989. x/189 pp. $12.95 pb.

Proportionately, this is one of the more substantial commentaries in the series. Beeby gives some helpful clues to using his commentary in the introduction. He reads the text as a Christian in a refreshing way. LM***

Craigie, P. C. *Twelve Prophets*. DSB. 2 vols. Westminster, 1985. ix/239 pp. $14.95 hb./$7.95 pb.

As in most series, the minor prophets get short shrift in terms of space. This does not mean the present commentary is worthless; Craigie is too insightful for that. It is only that it could be so much better if twice as many pages were allocated to the Minor Prophets. LM***

Harper, W. R. *Amos and Hosea*. ICC. T. and T. Clark, 1905. clxxxi/424 pp. $29.95.

Harper is very concerned to separate what he considers to be "authentic" Amos materials from later additions. He uses obsolete poetical criteria for emendation. In the introduction he places Amos and Hosea in a critically reconstructed history of prophetism, and gives a history of the composition of biblical literature. S***

Hubbard, D. A. *Hosea*. TOTC. Inter-Varsity, 1989. 234 pp. $14.95 hb./$8.95 pb.

Hubbard's commentary on Hosea is proportionately one of the most extensive in the series. His commentary on the fourteen chapters of Hosea is nearly as long as Baldwin's on 1 and 2 Samuel. Hubbard takes full advantage of this fact to provide a compellingly written, thoughtful analysis of Hosea's prophecy. Hosea is one of the more difficult books of the Bible to interpret. His commentary is based on sound scholarship and extensive research, but is extremely readable. LM****

Kidner, D. *The Message of Hosea*. BST. Inter-Varsity, 1981. 142 pp. $9.95 pb.

This volume is one of the most engaging in the series. Kidner with his usual skill combines scholarship, pastoral insight, and concern with a vital writing style. LM****

Limburg, J. *Hosea–Micah*. Interp. John Knox, 1988. 201 pp. $17.95 hb.

This readable commentary concentrates on themes in certain selected texts. Brief, but very stimulating. LM***

McKeating, H. *Amos, Hosea, Micah*. CBC. Cambridge, 1971. x/198 pp. $12.95 pb.

McKeating ably sets the eighth-century background to these three prophets. He takes a moderately critical approach, but is engaging and informative. LM****

Mays, J. L. *Hosea*. OTL. Westminster, 1969. x/190 pp. $15.95 hb.

Mays consciously concentrates on the theological meaning of the text to the subordination of philology, text, and other exegetical concerns. He comes from a moderately critical perspective. MS***

Stuart, D. *Hosea–Jonah*. WBC. Word, 1987. xlv/537 pp. $24.95 hb.

This is one of the best recent commentaries on the Minor Prophets. It is a must-buy for everyone who is preaching on these books. It is intelligently conservative and emphasizes theology without ignoring the other aspects of the text. Shows how these prophets operated in a tradition going back to the covenant curses of the Pentateuch. MS****

Wolff, H. W. *Hosea*. Hermeneia. Fortress, 1974. xxiii/259 pp. $24.95 hb.

Originally published in German in 1965, Wolff's work on Hosea has been the most influential force in Hosea studies for over two decades. This is an excellent commentary on all aspects of the text written from a critical perspective. MS****

Joel

Allen, L. C. *Joel, Obadiah, Jonah, and Micah*. NICOT. Eerdmans, 1976.

See under Jonah.

Craigie, P. C. *Twelve Prophets*. DSB. 2 vols. Westminster, 1985.

See under Hosea.

Finley, T. J. *Joel, Amos, Obadiah*. WEC. Moody, 1990. 417 pp. $25.95 hb.

This is a full-orbed commentary interested in all aspects of the biblical books which it studies. There are comments about history, literary matters, theology, philology, and practical application. Finley takes careful and reasoned positions. His writing style is clear and interesting. MS****

Hubbard, D. A. *Joel and Amos*. TOTC. Inter-Varsity, 1989. 245 pp. $14.95 hb./$8.95 pb.

This volume is brief, yet very useful—particularly in the areas of historical background, theology, and application. Well-written. LM****

Limburg, J. *Hosea–Micah*. Interp. John Knox, 1988.

See under Hosea.

Ogden, G. S., and R. R. Deutsch. *Joel and Malachi: A Promise of Hope, A Call to Obedience*. ITC. Eerdmans, 1987. x/120 pp. $7.95 pb.

These are competent, concise commentaries on two important Minor Prophets. Ogden and Deutsch appear to pay more attention to the contemporary relevance of the text—an announced intention of the series. LM***

Smith, J. M. P:, W. H. Ward, and J. H. Bewer. *Micah, Zephaniah, Nahum, Habakkuk, Obadiah and Joel*. ICC. T. and T. Clark, 1911.

See under Micah.

Stuart, D. *Hosea–Jonah*. WBC. Word, 1987.

See under Hosea.

Watts, J. D. W. *The Books of Joel, Obadiah, Jonah, Nahum, Habakkuk and Zephaniah*. CBC. Cambridge, 1975. x/190 pp. $10.95 pb.

There are short, helpful introductions to each book. Watts explores the connection between these books and the day of the Lord and worship themes. He argues that these prophecies are prophetic liturgies. LM***

Wolff, H. W. *Joel and Amos*. Hermeneia. Fortress, 1977. xxiv/392 pp. $29.95 hb.

This commentary was written originally in German in 1969 and is a benchmark study of both books. Written from a moderately critical perspective. MS****

Amos

Andersen, F. I., and D. N. Freedman. *Amos*. AB. Doubleday, 1989. xliii/977 pp.

This massive commentary is obviously not for those who are only casually interested in the Book of Amos. The incredible detail is especially welcomed by the scholar as well as the seminary student and studious pastor. The authors are explicit about their method and much can be carried over to the study of other biblical books. The commentary focuses on the final form of the text. It explains the changes in Amos's message by "dynamic developments in the prophet's career" rather than by a later editor who radically transforms his message. They do see evidence of editorial activity, but observe a "coherence between prophet and editor" (p. 74). There is a lot of information in this commentary. It is a must for those who really want to delve into the Hebrew text of Amos. MS*****

Craigie, P. C. *Twelve Prophets*. DSB. 2 vols. Westminster, 1985.

See under Hosea.

Harper, W. R. *Amos and Hosea.* ICC. T. and T. Clark, 1905.
See under Hosea.

Hubbard, D. A. *Joel and Amos.* TOTC. Inter-Varsity, 1989.
See under Joel.

Limburg, J. *Hosea–Micah.* Interp. John Knox, 1988.
See under Hosea.

McKeating, H. *Amos, Hosea, Micah.* CBC. Cambridge, 1971. x/198 pp.

See under Hosea.

Martin-Achard, R., and S. Paul Re'emi. *Amos and Lamentations.* ITC. Eerdmans, 1984. viii/134 pp. $10.95 pb.

Martin-Achard concentrates on exposition and social application. LM***

Mays, J. L. *Amos.* OTL. Westminster, 1969. 176 pp. $15.95 hb.

Mays provides an extensive treatment of the book from a moderately critical perspective. He presents philological and other technical analyses, but does not lose sight of the theological message of the book. MS****

Motyer, J. A. *Amos: The Day of the Lion.* BST. Inter-Varsity, 1974. 208 pp. $9.95 pb.

This volume, one of the first in the series, is well written by a competent and popular expositor. Although popular, it has substantial research behind it. LM***

Smith, G. V. *Amos: A Commentary.* Zondervan, 1988. 300 pp. $17.95 hb.

Smith has produced a magisterial treatment of the Book of Amos from an evangelical perspective. He exegetes the text with extensive treatment of text, philology, literary structure, and theological message. MS****

Stuart, D. *Hosea–Jonah.* WBC. Word, 1987.

See under Hosea.

Vawter, B. *Amos, Hosea, Micah, with an Excursus on Old Testament Priesthood.* OTM. Michael Glazier, 1981. 169 pp. $12.95 hb./$7.95 pb.

This volume is a well written and lucid presentation of three of the most prominent Minor Prophets and prophecy in general. Written from a critical perspective. LM***

Wolff, H. W. *Joel and Amos.* Hermeneia. Fortress, 1977.

See under Joel.

Obadiah

Allen, L. C. *Joel, Obadiah, Jonah, and Micah.* NICOT. Eerdmans, 1976.

See under Jonah.

Baker, D. W., T. D. Alexander, and B. K. Waltke. *Obadiah, Jonah, Micah.* TOTC. Inter-Varsity, 1988. 207 pp. $14.95 hb./$8.95 pb.

Baker wrote the section on Obadiah. He takes a highly competent, evangelical approach to the book, emphasizing historical background and theology. LM****

Coggins, R. J., and S. P. Re'emi. *Nahum, Obadiah, Esther: Israel among the Nations.* ITC. Eerdmans, 1985. x/140 pp. $7.95 pb.

These three books are presented as expressions of late attitudes toward the Gentile nations. The authors provide a competent interpretation from a moderately critical perspective. LM***

Craigie, P. C. *Twelve Prophets.* DSB. 2 vols. Westminster, 1985.

See under Hosea.

Eaton, J. H. *Obadiah, Nahum, Habakkuk, Zephaniah.* TBC. SCM, 1961. 159 pp.

Eaton identifies these prophets with temple service. He writes well and knowledgeably. LM***

Limburg, J. *Hosea–Micah.* Interp. John Knox, 1988.

See under Hosea.

Smith, J. M. P., W. H. Ward, and J. H. Bewer. *Micah, Zephaniah, Nahum, Habakkuk, Obadiah and Joel*. ICC. T. and T. Clark, 1911.

See under Micah.

Stuart, D. *Hosea–Jonah*. WBC. Word, 1987.

See under Hosea.

Watts, J. D. W. *The Books of Joel, Obadiah, Jonah, Nahum, Habakkuk and Zephaniah*. CBC. Cambridge, 1975.

See under Joel.

Wolff, H. W. *Obadiah and Jonah*. Augsburg, 1986.

See under Jonah.

Jonah

Allen, L. C. *Jonah, Obadiah, and Micah*. NICOT. Eerdmans, 1976. 427 pp. $24.95 hb.

Allen provides an up-to-date, insightful, and careful commentary on these interesting books. He writes with literary sensitivity, although many evangelicals will disagree with some of his conclusions. MS***

Baker, D. W., T. D. Alexander, and B. K. Waltke. *Obadiah, Jonah, Micah*. TOTC. Inter-Varsity, 1988.

T. D. Alexander wrote the section on Jonah. Like the other authors in the book, Alexander provides a very helpful guide to the historical background and theology of the book. Alexander also provides a very interesting discussion of the genre of the book and concludes that it is didactic history writing. LM****

Craigie, P. C. *Twelve Prophets*. DSB. 2 vols. Westminster, 1985.

See under Hosea.

Knight, G. A. F., and F. W. Golka. *The Song of Songs and Jonah*. ITC. Eerdmans, 1988.

See under Song of Songs.

Limburg, J. *Hosea–Micah*. Interp. John Knox, 1988.

See under Hosea.

Mitchell, H. G., J. M. P. Smith, and J. A. Bewer. *Haggai, Zechariah, Malachi, and Jonah*. ICC. T. and T. Clark, 1912. xxvi/362 + 88 +265 pp. $29.99 hb.

These are three volumes bound in one. All three authors provide classical critical studies of the most thorough kind. Technical and somewhat obsolete. S***

Stuart, D. *Hosea–Jonah*. WBC. Word, 1987.

See under Hosea.

Watts, J. D. W. *The Books of Joel, Obadiah, Jonah, Nahum, Habakkuk and Zephaniah.* CBC. Cambridge, 1975.

See under Joel.

Wolff, H. W. *Obadiah and Jonah.* Trans. M. Kohl. Augsburg, 1986. 191 pp. $23.95 hb.

Wolff combines excellent philological ability with theological insight to produce a very helpful commentary on these two prophetic books. His stance is moderately critical. The format of the commentary makes his comments easy to get at. Good textual criticism. MS****

Micah

Alfaro, J. *Micah: Justice and Loyalty.* ITC. Eerdmans, 1989. x/85 pp. $7.95 pb.

In keeping with the purposes of the series, Alfaro provides a third world reading of the prophet. He connects contemporary concerns with justice with the prophet's burning condemnation of the corrupt practices of his time. Moderately critical, this commentary, although brief, deserves reading because it provides a perspective to which many of us are oblivious. LM***

Allen, L. C. *Joel, Obadiah, Jonah, and Micah.* NICOT. Eerdmans, 1976.

See under Jonah.

Baker, D. W., T. D. Alexander, and B. K. Waltke. *Obadiah, Jonah, Micah.* TOTC. Inter-Varsity, 1988.

Waltke wrote the section on Micah. It is the distillation of careful scholarship presented in an engaging format for the layreader. LM*****

Craigie, P. C. *Twelve Prophets*. DSB. 2 vols. Westminster, 1985.

See under Hosea.

Hillers, K. *Micah*. Hermeneia. Fortress, 1984. 192 pp. $17.95 hb.

Hillers avoids redaction criticism as too speculative. He approaches the book as a whole rather than diachronically. He sees Micah's oracles as a part of a "revitalization" program. This program protests oppression and looks to a new age. Should be consulted by serious students. MS***

Limburg, J. *Hosea–Micah*. Interp. John Knox, 1988.

See under Hosea.

McKeating, H. *Amos, Hosea, Micah*. CBC. Cambridge, 1971. x/198 pp.

See under Hosea.

Mays, J. L. *Micah*. OTL. Westminster, 1976. xii/169 pp. $15.95 hb.

A rare one-volume commentary on Micah. This is a well written commentary that deserves close attention. Mays is a good scholar in the critical school. He communicates well and provides a well-rounded commentary. MS***

Smith, J. M. P., W. H. Ward, and J. H. Bewer. *Micah, Zephaniah, Nahum, Habakkuk, Obadiah and Joel.* ICC. T. and T. Clark, 1911. xix/537 pp. $19.95 hb.

These authors are clear in their writing and critical in their approach to these Minor Prophets. They give a detailed overview to historical background. Technical and dated. S***

Smith, R. L. *Micah–Malachi.* WBC. Word, 1984. xvii/358 pp. $22.95 hb.

This commentary is solid and competent. It is hampered by size restrictions. The section on Nahum, for example, is extremely scanty and not particularly original. LM**

Nahum

Achtemeier, E. *Nahum–Malachi.* Interp. John Knox, 1986. x/201 pp. $17.95 hb.

An insightful commentary from a moderately critical perspective. LM***

Baker, D. W. *Nahum, Habakkuk and Zephaniah.* TOTC. Inter-Varsity, 1988. 121 pp. $14.95 hb./$8.95 pb.

Baker's commentary shares the strengths of the series: engaging writing style and emphasis on theology and historical background. LM****

Boadt, L. *Jeremiah 26–52, Habakkuk, Zephaniah, Nahum.* OTM. Michael Glazier, 1982.

See under Jeremiah.

Coggins, R. J., and S. P. Re'emi. *Nahum, Obadiah, Esther: Israel among the Nations.* ITC. Eerdmans, 1985.

See under Obadiah.

Craigie, P. C. *Twelve Prophets.* DSB. 2 vols. Westminster, 1985.

See under Hosea.

Eaton, J. H. *Obadiah, Nahum, Habakkuk, Zephaniah.* TBC. SCM, 1961. 159 pp.

See under Obadiah.

Maier, W. A. *The Book of Nahum.* Concordia, 1959. 386 pp. $15.95 pb.

This massive commentary on the short Book of Nahum was written by a radio preacher from the Lutheran Church-Missouri Synod. While knowledgeable in matters concerning the Old Testament, Maier adopts unnecessarily polemical and rigidly conservative positions in the exegesis of the text—including some outlandish attempts to preserve the Masoretic Text. The commentary contains a lot of information, and raises the main issues of the book. It fails to provide the answers. LM***

Robertson, O. P. *The Books of Nahum, Habakkuk, and Zephaniah.* NICOT. Eerdmans, 1990. x/357 pp. $28.95 hb.

This commentary gives significant attention to three of the more interesting, but often neglected, Minor Prophets. Robertson excels in theological analysis and pastoral application. The commentary is weak in terms of philological and other technical studies. LM****

Smith, J. M. P., W. H. Ward, and J. H. Bewer. *Micah, Zephaniah, Nahum, Habakkuk, Obadiah and Joel.* ICC. T. and T. Clark, 1911.

See under Micah.

Smith, R. L. *Micah–Malachi.* WBC. Word, 1984.

See under Micah.

Watts, J. D. W. *The Books of Joel, Obadiah, Jonah, Nahum, Habakkuk and Zephaniah.* CBC. Cambridge, 1975.

See under Joel.

Habakkuk

Achtemeier, E. *Nahum–Malachi.* Interp. John Knox, 1986.

See under Nahum.

Baker, D. W. *Nahum, Habakkuk and Zephaniah.* TOTC. Inter-Varsity, 1988.

See under Nahum.

Boadt, L. *Jeremiah 26–52, Habakkuk, Zephaniah, Nahum.* OTM. Michael Glazier, 1982.

See under Jeremiah.

Craigie, P. C. *Twelve Prophets.* DSB. 2 vols. Westminster, 1985.

See under Hosea.

Eaton, J. H. *Obadiah, Nahum, Habakkuk, Zephaniah.* TBC. SCM. 1961. 159 pp.

See under Obadiah.

Robertson, O. P. *The Books of Nahum, Habakkuk, and Zephaniah.* NICOT. Eerdmans, 1990.

See under Nahum.

Smith, J. M. P., W. H. Ward, and J. H. Bewer. *Micah, Zephaniah, Nahum, Habakkuk, Obadiah and Joel.* ICC. T. and T. Clark, 1911.

See under Micah.

Smith, R. L. *Micah–Malachi.* WBC. Word, 1984.

See under Micah.

Szeles, M. E. *Habakkuk and Zephaniah: Wrath and Mercy.* ITC. Eerdmans, 1987. x/118 pp. $10.95 pb.

A helpful, competent study by a Romanian scholar. Unfortunately, she does not interact with her own society that much. She does set the books within their historical context. LM***

Zephaniah

Achtemeier, E. *Nahum–Malachi*. Interp. John Knox, 1986.

See under Nahum.

Baker, D. W. *Nahum, Habakkuk and Zephaniah*. TOTC. Inter-Varsity, 1988.

See under Nahum.

Craigie, P. C. *Twelve Prophets*. DSB. 2 vols. Westminster, 1985.

See under Hosea.

Eaton, J. H. *Obadiah, Nahum, Habakkuk, Zephaniah*. TBC. SCM, 1961. 159 pp.

See under Obadiah.

Robertson, O. P. *The Books of Nahum, Habakkuk, and Zephaniah*. NICOT. Eerdmans, 1990.

See under Nahum.

Smith, J. M. P., W. H. Ward, and J. H. Bewer. *Micah, Zephaniah, Nahum, Habakkuk, Obadiah and Joel*. ICC. T. and T. Clark, 1911.

See under Micah.

Smith, R. L. *Micah–Malachi*. WBC. Word, 1984.

See under Micah.

Szeles, M. E. *Habakkuk and Zephaniah: Wrath and Mercy.* ITC. Eerdmans, 1987. x/118 pp. $10.95 pb.

See under Habakkuk.

Watts, J. D. W. *The Books of Joel, Obadiah, Jonah, Nahum, Habakkuk and Zephaniah.* CBC. Cambridge, 1975.

See under Joel.

Haggai

Achtemeier, E. *Nahum–Malachi.* Interp. John Knox, 1986.

See under Nahum.

Baldwin, J. G. *Haggai, Zechariah, Malachi.* TOTC. Inter-Varsity, 1972. 253 pp. $14.95 hb./$8.95 pb.

A very insightful, conservative commentary. LM***

Boadt, L. *Jeremiah 26–52, Habakkuk, Zephaniah, Nahum.* OTM. Michael Glazier, 1982.

See under Jeremiah.

Craigie, P. C. *Twelve Prophets.* DSB. 2 vols. Westminster, 1985.

See under Hosea.

Meyers, C. L., and E. M. Meyers. *Haggai; Zechariah 1–8.* AB. Doubleday, 1987. 576 pp. $20.00 hb.

The Meyers treat Haggai and Zechariah 1–8 as not only stemming from the same period of time, but also being two parts of the same composite work. (They will treat the latter part of Zechariah along with Malachi in a subsequent commentary.) The Meyers are archeologists, and so their commentary is full of helpful historical and archeological comments. They include an excellent bibliography. MS****

Mitchell, H. G., J. M. P. Smith, and J. A. Bewer. *Haggai, Zechariah, Malachi, and Jonah*. ICC. T. and T. Clark, 1912.

See under Jonah.

Petersen, D. L. *Haggai and Zechariah*. OTL. Westminster, 1984. 320 pp. $24.95 hb.

Petersen and the Meyers have much in common in their approach to the text. They are both critical in their understanding of historical questions, but neither gets bogged down completely in such issues. Petersen is more interested in a positive interpretation of the books than in exhaustive interaction with the secondary literature. Like the Meyers, he does an admirable job reconstructing the historical, sociological, archeological, and economic background to the text. MS****

Smith, R. L. *Micah–Malachi*. WBC. Word, 1984.

See under Micah.

Struhlmueller, C. *Haggai and Zechariah*. ITC. Eerdmans, 1988. ix/165 pp. $10.95 pb.

This commentary is well informed and written with flair. Struhlmueller presents a moderately critical perspective that is concerned with present relevance. LM***

Verhoef, P. A. *The Books of Haggai and Malachi*. NICOT. Eerdmans, 1987. 384 pp. $24.95.

Verhoef is a South African scholar who is considerably at home in postexilic literature. He does a careful job of exegeting the Hebrew text. He also explores the theological message of Haggai and Malachi and traces their themes into the New Testament. This commentary is more academic in style than many others in the NICOT series; thus is it highly recommended as a scholarly guide to both of these prophetic books. MS***

Wolff, H. W. *Haggai*. Augsburg, 1988. 128 pp. $21.95 hb.

Wolff, as usual, is clear, concise, and insightful. He sees Haggai as a "model of communication." After all, Haggai was the one who got the Israelites to rebuild the temple. Analyzes the book as the result of three "growth rings": Haggai's proclamation, the work of a Haggai chronicler, and interpolations. MS****

Zechariah

Achtemeier, E. *Nahum–Malachi*. Interp. John Knox, 1986.

See under Nahum.

Baldwin, J. G. *Haggai, Zechariah, Malachi*. TOTC. Inter-Varsity, 1972.

See under Haggai.

Craigie, P. C. *Twelve Prophets*. DSB. 2 vols. Westminster, 1985.

See under Hosea.

Meyers, C. L., and E. M. Meyers. *Haggai; Zechariah 1–8.* AB. Doubleday, 1987.

See under Haggai.

Mitchell, H. G., J. M. P. Smith, and J. A. Bewer. *Haggai, Zechariah, Malachi, and Jonah.* ICC. T. and T. Clark, 1912.

See under Jonah.

Smith, R. L. *Micah–Malachi.* WBC. Word, 1984

See under Micah.

Struhlmueller, C. *Haggai and Zechariah.* ITC. Eerdmans, 1988.

See under Haggai.

Malachi

Achtemeier, E. *Nahum–Malachi.* Interp. John Knox, 1986.

See under Nahum.

Baldwin, J. G. *Haggai, Zechariah, Malachi.* TOTC. Inter-Varsity, 1972.

See under Haggai.

Craigie, P. C. *Twelve Prophets.* DSB. 2 vols. Westminster, 1985.

See under Hosea.

Kaiser, W. C. *Malachi: God's Unchanging Love*. Baker, 1984. 171 pp. $6.95 pb.

A practical commentary that combines scholarly tidbits with pastoral concern. The volume illustrates principles found in the author's *Toward an Exegetical Theology*. An appendix on how to use commentaries is included. LM***

Mitchell, H. G., J. M. P. Smith, and J. A. Bewer. *Haggai, Zechariah, Malachi, and Jonah*. ICC. T. and T. Clark, 1912.

See under Jonah.

Ogden, G. S., and R. R. Deutsch. *Joel and Malachi: A Promise of Hope, a Call to Obedience*. ITC. Eerdmans, 1987.

See under Joel.

Smith, R. L. *Micah–Malachi*. WBC. Word, 1984.

See under Micah.

Verhoef, P. A. *The Books of Haggai and Malachi*. NICOT. Eerdmans, 1987.

See under Haggai.

Appendix A

An Old Testament Library on a Budget

Books are increasingly expensive. Many people cannot afford "the best" on each biblical book. Seminary students and novice ministers find that they need a reference library, but cannot afford much while they are paying tuition or rearing a family. Most of the following suggestions come from the *Daily Study Bible* and the *Tyndale Old Testament Commentaries*. These are excellent sets for people on limited budgets, although they do not provide much of the information the more expensive volumes contain. These volumes are simply stop-gap for ministers while they build the reference library described below (the Ideal Old Testament Reference Library). Most laypeople will be satisfied with the "library on a budget."

It must be remembered that these are not the best commentaries on each book, but good, inexpensive ones which cover the whole Old Testament. The commentaries are simply listed here; descriptions may be found in the body of this book.

Kidner, D. *Genesis*. TOTC. Inter-Varsity, 1967. 224 pp. $14.95 hb./$8.95 pb.

Cole, R. Alan. *Exodus*. TOTC. Inter-Varsity, 1973. 239 pp. $14.95 hb./$8.95 pb.

Harrison, R. K. *Leviticus*. TOTC. Inter-Varsity, 1980. 252 pp. $8.95 pb.

Knight, G. A. F. *Leviticus*. DSB. Westminster, 1981. 173 pp. $12.95 hb./$6.95 pb.

Wenham, G. J. *Numbers*. TOTC. Inter-Varsity, 1981. 240 pp. $14.95 hb./$8.95 pb.

Payne, D. F. *Deuteronomy*. DSB. Westminster. $14.95 hb./$7.95 pb.

Auld, A. G. *Joshua, Judges, and Ruth*. DSB. Westminster, 1984. 290 pp. $15.95 hb./$6.95 pb.

Baldwin, J. *1 and 2 Samuel*. TOTC. Inter-Varsity, 1988. 299 pp. $14.95 hb./$8.95 pb.

Auld, A. G. *Kings*. DSB. Westminster, 1986. ix/259 pp. $15.95 hb./$8.95 pb.

McConville, J. G. *I and II Chronicles*. DSB. Westminster, 1984. 280 pp. $14.95 hb./$7.95 pb.

McConville, J. G. *Ezra, Nehemiah and Esther*. DSB. Westminster, 1985. xii/197 pp. $14.95 hb./$7.95 pb.

Baldwin, J. G. *Esther*. TOTC. Inter-Varsity, 1984. 126 pp. $14.95 hb./$8.95 pb.

Andersen, F. I. *Job*. TOTC. Inter-Varsity, 1976. 294 pp. $14.95 hb./$8.95 pb.

Kidner, D. *Psalms 1–72* and *Psalms 73–150*. TOTC. Inter-Varsity, 1973, 1975. x/492 pp. $14.95 hb./ $8.95 pb. (ea.).

Kidner, D. *Proverbs*. TOTC. Inter-Varsity, 1964. 192 pp. $14.95 hb./$8.95 pb.

Kidner, D. *A Time to Mourn and a Time to Dance*. Inter-Varsity, 1976. 110 pp. $9.95 pb.

Carr, G. L. *Song of Songs*. TOTC. Inter-Varsity, 1984. 175 pp. $14.95 hb./$8.95 pb.

Sawyer, J. F. A. *Isaiah*. DSB. 2 vols. Westminster, 1984, 1986. 280 pp. $14.95 hb./$7.95 pb.

Harrison, R. K. *Jeremiah and Lamentations.* TOTC. Inter-Varsity, 1973. 240 pp. $14.95 hb./$8.95 pb.

Craigie, P. C. *Ezekiel.* DSB. Westminster, 1983. x/321 pp. $14.95 hb./$7.95 pb.

Baldwin, J. G. *Daniel.* TOTC. Inter-Varsity, 1978. 210 pp. $14.95 hb./$8.95 pb.

Hubbard, D. A. *Hosea.* TOTC. Inter-Varsity, 1989. 234 pp. $14.95 hb./$8.95 pb.

Hubbard, D. A. *Joel and Amos.* TOTC. Inter-Varsity, 1989. 245 pp. $14.95 hb./$8.95 pb.

Craigie, P. C. *Twelve Prophets.* DSB. 2 vols. Westminster, 1985. ix/239 pp. $14.95 hb./$7.95 pb.

Motyer, J. A. *Amos: The Day of the Lion.* BST. Inter-Varsity, 1974. 208 pp. $9.95 pb.

Baker, D. W., T. D. Alexander, and B. K. Waltke. *Obadiah, Jonah, Micah.* TOTC. Inter-Varsity, 1988. 207 pp. $14.95 hb./$8.95 pb.

Baldwin, J. G. *Haggai, Zechariah, Malachi.* TOTC. Inter-Varsity, 1972. 253 pp. $14.95 hb./$8.95 pb.

Total cost (pb.) $222.85

Appendix B

The Ideal Old Testament Reference Library

This is it! If cost is no object, these are the books that (in my opinion) comprise the ideal Old Testament library. Do not shudder when you see the price tag. Rather, consider an investment over time. I have listed the books according to priority within categories. I realize that you will need to add books in other fields as well, especially New Testament commentaries and books on preaching and counseling. I hope I am not too prejudiced when I say that Old Testament commentaries and other reference books may be the most important part of your library because the Old Testament is more difficult for twentieth-century Christians to understand and apply to their lives.

In compiling this list, I had in mind the people who most often seek my advice on these matters—evangelical ministers and seminary students. Notice, for instance, that I am concerned to get an evangelical perspective on a subject up front, even if I have given the critical commentary higher marks above. Also, in this section I rarely suggest one of the budget books unless there is a real dearth of commentaries on a particular book. Nonetheless, they too are often a valuable addition to a library. I also do not include certain sets, but I have found that I use Keil and Delitzsch and Calvin all the time.

The books are here referred to only by the name of the author. The rest of the information may be found in the proper section above.

Introduction:	LaSor, Childs
Theology:	Robertson, Martens, Kaiser
History:	Merrill, Hayes/Miller
Atlas:	Either Beitzel, Pritchard, or Rasmussen (in that order)
Translation of Ancient Near Eastern Texts:	Pritchard, Coogan
Near Eastern History and Background:	Hallo, Oppenheim
Dictionaries and Other Hebrew Helps:	Holladay, Elwell, Harris, Even-Shoshan, Cowley (GKC), Waltke (in this case all of the above are helpful in different subcategories and are not listed by priority)
One-Volume Commentary:	Elwell

Commentaries

Genesis:	Wenham, Ross, Westermann, Sarna, Brueggemann
Exodus:	Childs, Durham, Gispen
Leviticus:	Wenham, Levine, Noordtzij
Numbers:	Wenham, Milgrom, Harrison, Budd
Deuteronomy:	Craigie, Ridderbos
Joshua:	Woudstra, Butler

Judges:	Goslinga, Boling, Auld
Ruth:	R. Hubbard
Samuel:	Gordon, Klein-Anderson, McCarter
Kings:	Hobbs, Nelson, Cogan/Tadmor
Chronicles:	Dillard, Williamson, Braun
Ezra–Nehemiah:	Williamson, Clines, Blenkinsopp, Fensham
Esther:	McConville, Baldwin
Job:	Clines, Pope, Hartley, Habel
Psalms:	Craigie, Allen, Kidner
Proverbs:	Kidner, McKane
Ecclesiastes:	Fox, Kidner, Crenshaw, Whybray
Song of Songs:	Pope, Carr
Isaiah:	Ridderbos, Oswalt, Watts, Young
Jeremiah:	Thompson, Clements, Holladay
Lamentations:	Hillers
Ezekiel:	Craigie, Blenkinsopp, Greenberg
Daniel:	Goldingay, Young, Ferguson, Towner
The Twelve:	(Since commentaries will sometimes include more than one Minor Prophet, these are listed by occurrence, not priority, in the above list. The first priority volumes, though, will be given an asterisk. If an author has more than one commentary on the Minor Prophets, the work will be cited in parentheses.)Limburg, Stuart*, Hubbard (*Joel and Amos*)*, Wolff (*Joel and Amos*), Allen*, Baker/Alexander/Waltke*, Wolff (*Obadiah and Jonah*), Achtemeier, Baker, Robertson*, Meyers/Meyers, Petersen, Verhoef.
Hosea:	D. Hubbard, Wolff, Andersen/Freedman
Amos:	Smith
Haggai:	Wolff

Total Price: Approximately $2700.00

Appendix C

Five-Star Commentaries

The following commentaries are given the highest ratings for each of the biblical books. These may not be the commentaries for you (for instance, they may be too technical or too critical), but they are the best because they accomplish their intentions from their own theological perspective most successfully.

Wenham, G. J. *Genesis 1–15.* WBC. Word, 1987. liii/353 pp. $24.95 hb.

Childs, B. S. *The Book of Exodus.* OTL. Westminster, 1974. xxv/659 pp. $27.95 hb.

Wenham, G. J. *The Book of Leviticus.* NICOT. Eerdmans, 1979. xiii/362 pp. $29.95 hb.

Milgrom, J. *Numbers.* JPS Torah Commentary. Jewish Publication Society, 1990. lxi/520 pp. $49.95.

Hubbard, R. L., Jr., *The Book of Ruth.* NICOT. Eerdmans, 1988. xiv/317 pp. $26.95 hb.

Dillard, R. B. *II Chronicles.* WBC. Word, 1987. xxiii/323 pp. $24.95 hb.

Williamson, H. G. M. *Ezra–Nehemiah*. WBC. Word, 1985. xix/428 pp. $14.95 hb.

Clines, D. J. A. *Job 1–20*. WBC. Word, 1989. cxi/501 pp. $24.99 hb.

Craigie, P. *Psalms 1–50*. WBC. Word, 1983. 375 pp. $22.95 hb.

Pope, M. H. *Song of Songs*. AB. Doubleday, 1977. xxi/743 pp. $22.00 hb.

Zimmerli, W. *Ezekiel 1 and 2*. Hermeneia. Fortress, 1979, 1982. xlvi/509 pp. xxxiv/606 pp. $39.95 hb. (ea.)

Goldingay, J. *Daniel*. Word, 1989. liii/351 pp. $24.95 hb.

Stuart, D. *Hosea–Jonah*. WBC. Word, 1987. xlv/537 pp. $24.95 hb.

Baker, D. W., T. D. Alexander, and B. K. Waltke. *Obadiah, Jonah, Micah*. TOTC. Inter-Varsity, 1988.